What Sh

The 6 Most Important Questions to Find Career Clarity, Growth, and Fulfillment.

By Rob Rando

Table of Contents

FOREWORD

How to Use this Guide

Question One: Am I bought in?

Question Two: Where can I find true enjoyment?

Question Three: How can I challenge myself to grow?

Question Four: What type of leader can I become?

Question Five: Where can I create synergy?

Question Six: How do I create lasting impact?

Final Thoughts

FOREWORD

Thank you for picking up a copy of What should I do next: The 6 most important questions to find Career Clarity, Growth, and Fulfillment. This is a follow up novel to The Happy Cog: The Happiness Guide working 9-5. In The Happy Cog I shared with my readers the methods and approach that I took to become a happier worker. Being a happy worker isn't about blind optimism or faking it until you make it, it's about finding something genuine. Over the course of writing that book I was able to find what truly made me happy at my job.

I learned how to be happy at a job I was previously miserable at. This was the same job that I was ready to walk away from just a few months prior. One day on vacation an insight came to me while I was quietly reflecting on the beach. It felt like I woke up because I realized how lucky I am to be able to afford this time off. I felt immense gratitude for the opportunity I was given.

I discovered was just how backwards my thinking was. It wasn't necessarily the job making me miserable; it was my approach to what I do every day. I treated it like a grind, so it became a grind.

Through consistent journaling, self-reflection, and a bit of experimentation I was able to discover what it was that lit me up at work. I found out parts that I liked about the company's mission. I opened my self-up to new connections and become a more enthusiastic version of myself. All of these shifts I went through gave me an opportunity to dive deeper and truly enjoy work more.

After seeing success both financially and emotionally with shifts in mindset, I decided that there was more I wanted to do.

There are points in our life where we seek growth. For some that growth is a constant motivator. I am one of those people. I realize that growth and a continued focused development truly makes me happy. While writing The Happy Cog I had started thinking about what was next for me to share. Now that I was in a much better place at work and the enjoying growth, I knew that I needed something new to keep up the same levels of enthusiasm.

I started thinking about the new role that I was in and the challenge I was given. Previously, I was responsible for a 200k/year quota and now I was expected to bring in 20+ million/year. Not only that, but I became responsible serving some of our company's most valuable key clients. The pressure to perform was instant.

Even though I was new on the team, I felt that with my prior experience and new-found motivation I could quickly work my way up to become a highly valued contributor. Then I started thinking beyond that. I started asking myself questions on how I could really step up to become more than average. I didn't just want to be valued, I wanted to help others feel good about what they do.

I made it a goal to find out exactly what questions I can ask to help others find true meaning and genuine happiness in their jobs. Systematically I created questions that would help people dig deep while also challenging them to go beyond themselves. I realized that I couldn't just create questions and expect someone to instantly be inspired. Instead I learned that the approach has to be well thought out or else the action steps are too great to overcome.

To do this I created a 6-step approach that felt authentic and actionable. Everything that I wrote in What should I do next? has been field tested and shared with those that I am closest with. I found out that by asking the right questions of others can help inspire them to think bigger. The most rewarding responses that I've received from these questions are when someone I admire and respect says "Wow, thank you, I never thought of it like that". Because I know that once someone knows what question to ask, they eventually find the exact answers that they need.

Like many writers, I reflect on my own personal experiences and obstacles. When I find out what works for me and I share it. However, I am not in the business of telling people what to do. The reason I wrote this book as an actionable guide is to help others them find their own answers.

The thing about life and being an individual is that we are all so very different. Each of us has access to a completely unique life experience. We have subtle nuances to our personality, strengths, weaknesses, and a countless combinations of character traits. Every one of us has the potential to be the greatest version of ourselves that we can be. If we do it right, we can inspire others to do the same. One day when all of us are working toward our highest selves the world becomes a happier place. That's when we can create global change.

The books I write are guides. They are guides to help you unlock your own potential. This book is no different.

In this title, What should I do next? The 6 most important questions to find Career Clarity, Growth, and Fulfillment. I am going to share with you a set of steps which are effectively guide posts to help you advance your career.
☐

How to use this guide

This book was written in a specific way that promotes focused thinking, deep self-reflection, and creativity. It's true that we are always thinking, in fact some experts 'estimate' that we have 50,000+ thoughts a day. Using the prompts in this book as a guide, you can center your thinking in a very pointed way. Self-reflection on its own is valuable tool. It helps us learn from mistakes as well as recognize patterns. Many of the steps we are going to look at in this book are going to be new, but familiar. The novelty of looking at old things in a new way sparks a certain kind of creative type spirt.

When we ask the right questions in the right way, we will find the right answers.

While putting this guide together, I thought about what questions I could ask that would help those reading getting more motivated, find more meaning, and take real action steps to progress their careers. I asked these same questions of myself to move up from a position with a $200,000 yearly quota to a role with a higher salary, larger commission and responsibility for managing accounts worth over 20 million dollars a year.

Inside we are going to look at the 6 areas you need to figure out to re-ignite the fire of ambition that creates positive change. At the same time, we are going to explore the practical but fulfilling action steps we need to take to move forward.

Each area we explore is another step on our path to reach our highest potential. First, we must start identifying the of basics of alignment to where we are with where we want to be. Then we are going to learn how we can cultivate more enjoyment right here and now. Next, we are going to take our current skills to the next level. Lastly, we are going to think bigger to the point where we stretch beyond what currently know.

The 6 fundamental questions that need to be asked are:
Question 1: Am I bought in?
Question 2: Where can I find true enjoyment?
Question 3: How can I challenge myself to grow?
Question 4: What type of leader can I become?
Question 5: Where can I create synergy?
Question 6: How do I create lasting impact?

Each chapter is dedicated to expounding upon then answering these key questions. One of the most powerful parts of each chapter are where we dissect these questions further into "guiding questions". These will truly help you grow if you take the time to answer each one. Although you may not have all of the insights at first, simply spending time reflecting on the question will eventually give you the answer you need. Not to worry though, each one of the guiding questions will have explanations that will help you to think about them in a new way.

Finally, at the end of each focus area there are actions steps that you can take that will give you tangible results in the real world. By answering the questions, then taking the practical steps you will be making a real difference with the people around you. The suggested action steps can be found in the "Actions and Habits" section at the end of each chapter. They are meant to be a bit challenging. This is where the progress happens.

It makes sense to start thinking about the questions as you read, letting your brain unlock insights naturally then go back and have a document of all the answers in one place.

You can find additional tools and resources such as PDFs/Activity sheets at PinegroveZen.com/tools.

Thank you and Enjoy!

Question One: Am I bought in?

The very first step to unlocking that part of ourselves that makes us feel alive is to align with our working environment. We must possess a certain level of 'buy-in' if we want to progress with authentic enthusiasm. It's important that we first understand our personal level of 'buy-in' before we can really dive into the essential inner work. In other words, we must believe that we are in a place that growth can happen.

The path to the top will be filled with challenges. As we become better versions of ourselves, we become capable of more and more things. Each stage of our progress is filled with tasks that we've never before encountered. Ideally along the way we are developing ourselves into the type of person that can handle the new situations that have been set before us. With all of that being said, the wrong work environment can absolutely impede on the personal progress that we've set out to make.

Buy- In, Definition: The definition of a buy-in is an agreement to do something, even though the person agreeing didn't have anything to do with the project beforehand.

As a member of an organization such as a company, your purpose is to help the group move forward in a particular direction. The particular direction in which you are moving is not necessarily your choice. This lack of choice can be frustrating, but only if it goes against your core beliefs. If you find that you can agree with the general motives of your organization, you will be able to adapt to the challenges that will occur on your journey. Most importantly your buy-in to the mission at hand creates an authentic desire to 'be better'.

The vision for the company is usually determined by a couple of individuals or a group of key decisions makers. Are these leaders of your company making decisions that you can be proud of? Are they good people? Do they care about others? These are the type of questions we need to ask as individual contributors. The more you care about what you do the easier it is to find a passion for your work.

You will find that some don't ever think about this aspect of their jobs. That's fine. However, if you have picked up this book, the assumption is you have aspiration to move beyond "this job". You are the type of person that knows how important it is to find the joy each and every single day. Part of finding that connection is to do the work to uncover it.

The reason that Buy in is so important is because without it you are at risk of blindly following. A blind follower is someone that takes orders without knowing their role in the bigger picture. It's like rowing a boat with a blindfold and letting somebody else steer. All of that effort needs to have a destination worth reaching. You must take off the blindfold and see where it is you are heading. We can do that by asking a set of guiding questions that illuminates the path ahead of us.

A responsible person creating his or her own fate, must question who they work for and the larger mission they are a part of. Then, you as an individual has to decide if the people you serve align with your values. Lastly, you must believe that the direction of your organization is the same one that you want to go.

That is not to say that current circumstances can't improve. In fact, we will explore how we can alter the direction in later chapters. We first must know that we are in good company.

Another way to look at this is how much excitement you can create around the product or service your company offers. If you can find genuine excitement about who it is your company serves (It's customers), then you can find enough reason to commit and 'buy-in'.

Now let's dig into guiding questions around buy-in, which you can answer for yourself. Reflecting on these questions will allow you to see the bigger picture. Also, you will be able to see through to the top and be confident in the direction you are heading in.

At the end of this section, there will be a set of challenges to put these questions into practice.

Guiding Questions on Buy-In

How strongly do you connect with your company's mission?

Before we go deep into our own personal growth, we must define our opportunities on a deeper level. Defining our company's mission is essential for us to analyze our own personal buy-in. At a basic level we want to be able to have a general agreement with the purpose of our employer. We are not just pieces of machinery that are plugged in. We are living, thinking, breathing people. It is our job to ask ourselves if we believe in what we are doing.

What does the organization we work for care about? Who do they serve? All of these ingredients give us the clues we need to get to the heart of our company's defining purpose.

Once we take the time to re-assess what is our company does, what they care about, and who they serve we go back to the original question "How strongly do you connect with your company's mission?" What we need to look for in order to answer this question is something we will call alignment. Ideally, we want to strongly connect with every single facet of our employers' grand mission. At a minimum we need to feel connected to at least some part of what it is we do every day.

Now consider what it is your company does? In other words, think about all of the products or services that they offer. Where is your connection to what they produce? Would you be an avid user of the product or service if you didn't work for them? What about if someone pitched you the idea for this product of service, do you think you would of 'bought in'? What we are trying to determine here is if you feel enthused about the product or service that you are helping to bring to the world. If you aren't it makes it so much harder to show up with passion each and every day.

We then consider what does the company care about? For example, lets assume you are highly sensitive to the impact that you make on the environment. Every day in your life you make small personal decisions that can reduce your carbon footprint. You are super careful about re-using what you can and recycling what you can't. With all of that being said, it would make sense that you hold the company you work for to a similar standard. If one of your biggest core values is environmental impact, but the company you work for dumps hazard wastes into a nearby lake, its going be really hard for you to feel good about yourself each and every day. The organization you work for doesn't have to care about the exact same things for you to be happy. However, the more you can find areas that support your values the easier it will be for you step into bigger leadership roles.

Finally, who is it your company serves? Alternatively, who are the individuals that we (as a company) are helping with our products or services? Are you able to connect with your customers in an authentic way? You may not be a user of your organization's product or service, but that doesn't mean you can't build meaningful relationships with those that you serve. To be able to show up with a long-term deeply meaningful drive you want to have some connection to your customers. A connection could be as simple as you understanding how valuable what you do is to your customers. This internalized belief alone could give you the motivation necessary to be your best as often as possible. When you have a connection to the people you serve, you automatically start to figure out how you can do it better.

One of our goals is to be happy at work. Asking these types of questions allow you to really see what it is that resonates with you.

The final aspect of finding a connection to your organization's mission is to think about what direction they are heading in? Just as important as where your organization is where they are going. If your intention is to become a leader, you must know where you will be leading to. In a sense the destination and future of the company has already been laid out. With a mission in place, the general direction of the organization's future plan has been shared.

Change is hard. If buy-in means helping the organization to reach the next step in its evolution, you have to believe in where the company is moving. The actual direction of the company is much more nuanced and should be explored and contemplated before making a quick decision.

In all honesty if you are excited about the products and services that your organization provides, that can be enough to invest in its future. One of the easiest measurements of buy in is your excitement to talk about work. you are excited to talk about work. This will come into play later when talking about personal happiness as well. If you genuinely enjoy chatting about your job, company, and what is you do. You are probably in the right place.

Are you being led by the right people?
-Are the leaders competent, genuine, caring?
-Do you see people ahead of you as role models?
-Do you respect them?

A strong company is filled with strong leaders, there is no exception to that. Without the right combination of people and personalities in managing positions it is very difficult for an organization to stay on the right path. If we see the mission as the general direction of the company, we can look at the leadership as the drivers. They are the ones that are steering teams to the destination that was set forth. The greatest leaders are those who are able to help others feel motivated and connected to their work.

The individuals who are given the authority to lead must also be aligned with a mission for them to also continue to work with passion and purpose. It is a true joy working for men and woman that feel a deep meaning for what is that they do. Even if you don't particularly like some of the people in charge, those that care about the work will always have an advantage over apathetic leaders.

As hard as it is to believe the wrong people sometimes get selected for leadership roles. This could be due to politics, flashes of brilliance, or poor talent evaluation. Regardless the ones that suffer the most are the employees that have to report to these individuals. This is also one of the biggest causes of resentment in an organization. Bad leadership creates toxicity throughout teams with a constant critical undertone.

It's important for those of us who are striving to progress in our careers to know who will be on our team at the next level. As we will see in later chapters to really excel you will need to be able to work across departments with leaders of all styles. At a very base level, a good leader will have an understanding of the priorities and projects of other teams within the organization.

One of the easiest ways to know that this is the right company for you is your level of admiration for those put in charge. When you look around your organization who are the people who have been selected for management roles? Are they the right fit? Have they been selected from merit or other factors?

The reason why these questions are so important for overall buy-in is because you can see how committed your organization is to putting the right people in place. The right individuals selected for the right job makes a vast difference in the overall happiness of employees. On the other side of the equation, having the right leaders in place will make it much more likely that the company reaches its current and future financial goals.

When you look at those who are in positions of authority, ask yourself of are you impressed with them? More specifically, is what they are doing inspiring you to 'step it up' in some way or form. If the answer is yes, this is usually a good sign that you are in a good organization. When your personal view of leaders is that they are people you want to be like, consider this is a strong positive sign for buy-in. Use this observation as a reframe to be more like them.

What is that you can do to be like those that you highly respect within the organization? More to come on this later.

Sure, there could be a few managers and higher that you particularly don't respect, but if this is prevalent throughout the company it may be hard to genuinely want to move up in that organization.

Actions and Habits: Buy-In

The Action and Habits section is where you can take real steps to fully absorb the material we just reflected on. These habits and activities are meant to compliment the reflective thinking from the previous section. Now that we have taken the time to ask ourselves powerful questions, we can motivate ourselves to take actions that help us progress.

These steps along with a PDF with all of the chapter's questions can be downloaded at Pinegrovezen.com/Tools

Buy-In Habit 1: Establish a Pattern of Good Behavior

After you have taken the time to reflect on the questions about your personal sense of buy-in, you should have a better idea if this is the right place for you. If you have decided that you are at least partially bought, you are going to want to start implement habits that reflect the way you feel.

Habits we do at work consistently will show others that we are committed and connected to what we do. Integrating these traits will turn us into better leaders that others will want to follow.

<u>Habit: Establish a Pattern of Good Behavior</u>. To make this concept something that can be actionable you should be doing the right things consistently.

What are the right things? While simple and obvious – this mindset can be overlooked. The right things are working when it's time to work, doing a good job consistently, and having a good attitude.

Work when it's time to work. A small and simple habit shift that can result in a life time of good discipline. When you get in, get settled and get to work. Do your job and take pride in doing it well. In some environments you may be able to get away with not working too hard while doing just enough to get buy. But if you want to truly connect beyond that, you must do the work. Do it well and do it consistency. When personal pride plays a part in how you do your job, you will see a lot more productivity and so will others around you.

Have a good attitude. This can be hard. There are times regardless of how much buy-in you have
that situations exist that just don't sit well with you. It's ok to have a bit of an edge. In fact, an edge makes you unique and gives you some bite which can be great things for getting things done with vigor.
However, part of establishing a good behavior habit is showing up with the attitude that we are in this
together.

Don't take frustrations out on other people or managers. Work with them to figure out better
ways. Sure, voice your frustration but do it in the most tactfully way you can. All the while continue to show up in way that is productive. This good habit of doing the work regardless of how you feel validates you in a powerful way when you do speak up in frustration. Conversely, constantly complaining leads to others to not take your complaints seriously.

Keep this in mind. If the people around you seem to avoid you or not engage with you when you 'complain', this may be a sign that you need to adjust your attitude. Negativity can sneak up on us.

To summarize:
Do what is asked of you with a good attitude. It will make a significant difference in the respect and engagement you receive from your peers.
Be consistent in your effort
Work hard, and work with pride

Buy-In Habit 2: Understand the long-term vision of the company

Part of becoming more connected with what you do is having an interest in long term strategies. These are the decisions that are sometimes made behind closed doors (depending on your current level). When leadership teams get together, they are often focused on where they are, but more importantly where they need to go to stay competitive. The immediate and long-term focus set forth by leadership determines what actions employees will have to take.

It can be hard for you to feel connected to your work if you are treated as simple a cog in the machine. The way to get past all of that is to learn to care about strategy. Even though you may not be part of the group that is setting the strategic vision (yet), you can still dig deeply into where your company is going. This will allow you to understand a bit more about why you are doing what you are doing. Most of all it helps you develop a strong why behind the actions that you take every day.

<u>Have a good understanding of both 1 year and 5 years plans.</u> The idea behind getting acquainted with short- and long-term plans is for you to think beyond your role. One of the reasons many of us feel so unencouraged by our work is because we don't feel connected to it. Part of that lack of connection comes from no tie in to the bigger picture. To encourage an attitude shift towards more meaningful work, we must integrate with the strategy in our own unique way.

The task here is to develop your own understanding what the organization's direction is for the next 12 months. Then further out, figure out where leadership is steering the ship. A lot of the 1- and 5-year plans are clearly articulated in many organizations. However, what we want to do is create our own understanding of it.

<u>Figure out how well the plan is being executed</u>. This might take some research. It may even take meetings with the right people. What you should be doing as a future leader in the organization is training yourself in the art of execution. One way to do that in your current position is to measure progress against the strategy that has been laid out before you. A mission statement is one thing, but there are long term strategies that are being discussed and rolled out in one way or another. You may not be at the level where you can find a direct answer, but can you see what's happening through the actions that are being taken.

Think about where the hiring focus has been in the past 6 months. Do you see areas of growth in certain departments? What about those companywide 'stand-ups' or announcements? What is the focus of those all hands-on deck presentations?

What you will be doing is simply trying to identify patterns. The key here is to see if the actions are lining up with what is being share with you

Question Two: Where can I find true enjoyment?

Success can be measured in several ways. If our goal is to be happy in life, then we need to start setting metrics around that goal. Often, we mistakenly measure our success by what we 'think' success should look like.

Use this moment to define your own success by asking yourself 'what makes me happy'. It doesn't have to be all about achievement. Concentrating on how we want to feel instead of 'what we want' could make all of the difference. When we set metrics that really matter to us, we take actions that truly fulfill us.

Finding true enjoyment at the place you work will be the focus of this section. Being happy at a place where we spend 1/3 of our lives should be a goal. Of course, as we begin to work harder there will be struggles that we will face. Part of learning to find joy in your work is developing a strong mindset around challenges.

Here is the thing about true enjoyment. It can't be faked. However, it can be discovered. The topic of my first book was exactly how to approach your work life to find the true enjoyment. If interested, please find and download a copy of The Happy Cog on Amazon Kindle.

When uncovering true enjoyment, we are looking for a couple of things. First, we are learning to identify what we are really good at. Doing things, we are already good at creates opportunity for the highest states of flow. Secondly, we are digging into where we get energized. This means discovering the tasks you already do that effectively give you more energy. By knowing what gives us energy, we can create more of it which makes everything else we have to do that much easier. Lastly, as we become more self-aware, we are going to dig more into 'fit'. What this means is asking yourself if you are doing work that is going to allow you to grow into your full potential.

Within a given day there are several tasks that we must do for a job well done. The reality is
some of the responsibilities we have are better suited to our core strengths. If we are lucky, the responsibilities of our role align directly with our personal motivations. The happiest and most productive workers see their jobs as extensions of themselves.

Work happiness and energy are closely tied together. When you are happy you are more energized to work on tasks. Inversely, when you have energy you are likely to be happier working on the tasks in front of you. To cultivate this relationship more intentionally you should be trying to discover which areas of your role do energize you.

If you are still in the early stages of your career it's very possible that you are still figuring out what you like and don't like. Even if you end creating a business out of a specific passion there will still be challenging parts of your work that you don't particularly enjoy.

The key here is to first understand what it is you like. Then to intentionally create a schedule to maximize the time you spend doing tasks and activities that you enjoy. The result of setting up your day like this is that you are better able to execute on all tasks. When we are intentional with how we spend our time, we are able to generate more energy. Achieving higher emotional states makes it easier to come up with insights, be productive, and find meaning in our work.

In the next set of questions, we are going to be asking ourselves questions that will help us create more energy. The following questions may challenge you to think about the role you're in. Previously, the chapter on buy-in was about the bigger picture. Now with these questions we will be focusing in on our personal beliefs. We need to discover happiness to be successful and move up to the next level.

Guiding Questions on True Enjoyment

What are your strengths?

One of the best questions a manager can ask his/her employees is to identify their strengths. Our strengths are what give us a uniqueness that can set us apart from others. A beautiful thing happens when a leader can get a team of employees operating with their highest potential.

Asking this question of yourself regularly allows you to bring your individual powers to the surface more often. Sometimes this question is hard to answer because of the nature of what we call a "strength". Often a trait that others would consider a strength is overlooked because it comes so naturally to us.

For example, you might be a naturally reflective person that recollects on your interactions through the week. Identifying a quiet trait like 'reflectiveness' is a power that could be used to better understand the customer experience. Another use case is the ability to look back on past projects, a reflective person may be able to better assess where things went wrong, or where things went right. With a little bit of focus and adjustment on job related tasks, reflectiveness could become an identifiable strength.

It is tricky to dig deep and figure out what we are strong at because not all strengths are touted equally in society. We are influenced by what society seems to value. As Susan Cain points out in her book Quiet, "outward confidence and extroversion is regularly pushed on us as the only way for leadership, but what studies show is introverts are better at developing expertise." This concept broadly applied to strength seeking lets us creatively find advantages that would be unique to us.

As with all tough questions, the answers don't always come flying out of us. It would be great if they would. Instead we must simply ask ourselves the question and let it stew for a while. The more you ask yourself about what you are strong at, the more often it is at top of mind. When we give powerful questions a more permanent part of our internal dialogue it allows us to find answers when we least expect it

A fantastic habit to develop up for self-reflection is journaling.

An Excerpt from The Happy Cog - Journaling is a method that allows our minds to focus energy in a very specific way. Writing is essentially the act of taking all of the thoughts floating around in our heads and pulling out the ones we want to specifically focus on.

By taking those thoughts and shining a conscious light on them, you can dictate which ones you want to bring to the surface. Journaling just to journal is better than nothing, but doing it in a strategic way is even more impactful.

The question "What are your strengths?" gives us an opportunity to remember what is that we are good at. It's very possible that we have strengths that use every day, but don't notice because we've never taken the step back to ask.

There are so many areas that you may naturally excel at, but take for granted. Think about tasks that colleagues seem to have a harder time with than you. Perhaps, there is a common grumbling amongst other team members about something you don't particularly have a problem with. It is likely that you don't feel have the same struggles as others because you compensate with your unique strengths.

Never take what comes easy to you for granted. Anything that comes natural to you could be a real struggle for somebody else. Know this and identify what it is that makes you uniquely powerful.

What parts of the job energize you?

Self-Awareness is one of the most rewarding abilities you can develop. Do you wake up excited every day to go to work and get started on your next project? Its ok if you don't, but could you imagine what it would be like. Could you picture a life where you wake up in the morning genuinely excited and even passionate about what you do for a living?

This is what this question is about. It's about understanding that every role is going to have its ups and downs. To really start to enjoy what we do, we need to identify what it is that energizes us. Depending on our current mindset it's possible that there is a fog clouding our vision of what it is we like to do.

To identify what gives you energy at work the first step is creating more self-awareness. A good way to go about this is to start creating a daily to do list, or an agenda. The reason we want to do this is to start to get an idea of what it is that energizes us.

Think about it like this: When you start a new work day, there are several things that you must get done. It's the nature of work there is always stuff that has to get done. To create more self-awareness, write down the tasks that you have to get done for the day. Also, if there are any items that you want to get done put those on the list as well.

As you go through your day put a check mark if you complete the task. If you complete a task and feel that you did it really well put a check mark and a plus sign. For tasks that you completed, did really well, and felt a genuine enjoyment put a check mark and 2 plus symbols. Lastly, if there are tasks that you didn't enjoy, but got done any way put a check and a minus symbol.

After doing this for a week or two you will start to see some patterns emerging. Those tasks that regularly receive a check plus are the ones you should pay attention to. These are the activities that align with what you like to do. To get the most out every day it is your responsibility to uncover the parts of your job that you genuinely enjoy and excel at.

As you start to pay attention you will notice there are certain parts of the job that drive you. Be especially cognizant of anything you do that you also look forward to. The aspects of our role that truly gives us energy makes everything else we have to do that much easier.

How much better would your working life be if you could do more of what makes you happy? That's essentially what we are doing when we are answering this question. We are finding out what it is that gives us enthusiasm. We are asking this question to find out what makes us feel more alive. To prevent any type of burn out we must do our best to stay inspired and motivated in some way. Our other option is let the days pass with nothing to show for it.

I myself went through this process when I was facing adversity at work. I was in a sales role that involved 85% prospecting for new leads via cold calling and/or emails. As many in sales know one of the essential keys of success is activity. The other caveat sometimes not mentioned is the that the energy your brining behind the activity matters. 25 quality reach outs with confident and focused message are better than 50 calls that are unenthusiastic and uninspired.

I started to notice that in the morning I had the right stuff. I set out to make an impact in the early parts of the day. I had a good routine at this point so I was able to come into work energized and ready to go. I would book myself a quiet room and hit the phones for the next 2 hours or so. My calls in the morning were good. I would make connections and felt good.

When it came to the afternoon the attempts to keep up the same activity were futile. I would make calls, but my energy was drained. I just couldn't set appointments as easily as I did in the morning. In fact, it was much harder. My whole being dragged through the second half of the day. The poor people I had to reach out to noticed it too.

After weeks of this I decided I needed to step back. I realized I was wasting half a day with this method. The pattern that I observed was that I was great at prospecting in the morning and awful at it in the afternoon. However, if there was a call or meeting scheduled in the afternoon, I could take the time to prepare. The preparation I did led to really productive sales presentations. There it was I thought "prospect hard in the morning, and set up presentations in the afternoon". This insight let me to restructure how I approached my day.

The shift I made was push out my mornings as long as possible. This meant I had a big breakfast and when I got into the office I worked on prospecting or some form of outreach until 1:30 – 2:00pm. For any meetings, I would intentionally schedule later in the day so I could prepare for them better. This change in habit led to a huge increase in energy. I knew which tasks I handled best and when. Activities that were previously difficult became much easier to accomplish because I did them when I was in the right 'zone'.

Understanding where your energy comes from is one thing, but it is just as important knowing what drains you. The parts of the job that sap your energy are equally as important to be aware of. If we want to be the most effective version of ourselves at work, we should know what our kryptonite is.

Referring back to our do lists and the check + or check – marks, we should notice that there are some tasks that are consistently negative.

The tasks that are constantly a struggle to get done or feel like a grind are the energy drainers. Energy drain happens when there are parts of a role that don't align well with our strengths or passions. We have trouble finding a greater connection behind these tasks which makes motivation difficult. You may not be able to entirely eliminate these activities at first but knowing what these tasks are will help you to better structure your day.

When you know what parts of the job energize you, you will be able to create more opportunities. There is a magical thing that happens when you are intentional with your daily structure. You create more joy and enthusiasm. By keeping tabs on what gives you energy, you can booster the other activities in your day.

Is this the right role for you?

The phrase "love what you do and you'll never have to work a day in your life" rings true. While even dream jobs can have challenges if you love what you do waking up for work is that much easier. Part of loving what you do is really knowing if the role you're in is right for you.

The question presented "Is this role right for you?" is about introspection of one's strengths, weaknesses, desires, and ambitions. What we really want to understand here is if what we do aligns with what we want. Keep in mind roles don't have to be perfect (and they rarely are). At a base level a job has to have the right DNA for us to grow into it and eventually excel.

For most of us, we start our careers with a limited set of options. The reality is most people aren't top tier Harvard graduates that get to choose a job of our choice. No, for many the start of our career comes from a smaller pool of options. In most circumstances, looming bills and the pay back of loans doesn't allow us to be picky. We may end up choosing a job that doesn't suite us entirely. The role we start with may lead us down a path doesn't align with our internal ambitions. Years later we may find ourselves in a job that leaves us feeling flat, unmotivated, or lost entirely.

The reason why so many feel a lack in their careers is because they are in roles that don't align with their values, strengths, or passions. We humans are a complex species. There is more to life than working. A lot more. There are things that we care about. Ideally, you should identify what it is you care about and measure that against what you do every day. At a minimum there should be some level of connection between the jobs we do and what is important to us. A strong misalignment can weigh heavily on the joy we experience at our jobs. This is why answering this specific question is so important. Is this role right for us?

What we are really trying to uncover is if we are somewhat emotionally connected to what we do every day. Do you like talking to people about your products? If you do, it's important that you get the opportunity to do so. Are you someone that sees themselves as creative? If you are, it's vital that you have enough autonomy to do things your own way once in a while.

Not every element of your current job is going to be perfect. Even the perfect job may lose its luster after initial novelty wears off.

Part of answering this question is finding out if what you do is the right level of challenge for your skill set. The idea of challenges meeting skill level is a well-studied concept called "flow" (check out Mihaly Csikszentmihalyi's Flow for more). A great role should generate more moments of than frustration.

Evaluate further by asking yourself "Do I have the necessary skills to do this job well?". Naturally, we are happier when are able to perform at a high level. Conversely, when we are in a position that greatly exceeds our current skill level overwhelm can take hold. These evaluations are important because to make it to the next level we have to make the right choices. 'Know Thyself' may be a cliched term, but the thing about clichés is they resonate with lots of people for long periods of time.

It shouldn't be too much to ask that the role we are in has more good elements to it then bad. However, it's important to remember the color of lens you are doing your evaluations in. There are times when we are so frustrated with work in general that everything is bad. Our attitudes can affect the outcome of what we measure. Keep that in mind when you are asking yourselves these questions. There is always room for improvement. With a base level of acceptance established we can start doing things that can propel us from an average worker to an above average leader.

Another way to evaluate if this is the right role comes down to one simple feeling. Do you feel important? If not then you need to find out if that's because of your perspective or if there is some reality to that statement. At the end of the day we have roles within companies because it up to us to fulfill a special need of the business. We are hired because of what we can contribute to the overall mission of the company. What we do day to day should at the very least feel like it matters.

In all honesty you wouldn't be around collecting paychecks if your company didn't value in some way. However, if we want to experience more joy at work we need to really see/feel the importance ourselves. This ties back to chapter one's question "Do you believe in the mission" because if you do it's much easier for you to feel like a valuable part of the machine.

Is it possible to create a new position for myself?

One of the ways we can experience more joy at work is to create it. To take the concept further allow yourself to believe in the possibility of creating the perfect role for yourself. The only way to do this is to have a strong self-awareness of what you would actually enjoy doing. Creating a position doesn't necessarily mean that your job title changes, but what you do day to day does. Imagine if you could design your job in a way that you are still doing what is required of you but you happen to like doing those activities. That is really a perfect scenario.

Awareness is so vital because it is the first step to improving your current situation. You must know what you are good at as well as what energizes you. Without this knowledge you won't be able to conjure up the ideal role for yourself.

After you've determined these two aspects of yourself you can start looking for opportunities within the organization. These opportunities could be operational gaps, market deficiencies or processes within your team that could be improved. Perhaps there is something that you do better than anyone else on the team. Could you trade one task out in favor of this more fulfilling task? It doesn't hurt to ask and the only way to ask well is to really think about it.

Pro Tip: Any time you are approaching leadership or your superiors about making a possible change you must prepare. There is no question that asking is the most important. Equally as important is to prepare for any conversation and objections beforehand. Prepping allows you form well-articulated points and counterpoints that may come up in any conversation. You should realize going in that you may not get what you want. That's ok you aren't going to win every battle. You aren't always going to get your way. These conversations that you have in your career aren't all or nothings. When making a new ask of someone the first few times can be equated to planting a seed. What we are doing here is brining awareness to the surface that we are looking to do more.

Actions and Habits: Find Enjoyment

The Actions and Habits to Implement section is this meant to compliment the reflective thinking done when answering each chapter's questions. These habits are actionable steps that you can take to make real progress toward advancing your career, or in this case your enjoyment of work.

These steps along with a PDF with all of the chapter's questions can be downloaded at PinegroveZen.com/Tools

Enjoyment Habit 1: Create more opportunity to do the activities that energize you.

For more enjoyment throughout our work days there is one thing we must do. We must find out what types of activities give us the most energy and then create time for those specific activities. There is so much variance about the types of jobs we have. Work becomes so much easier if we can find the tasks that we really enjoy and then make more time for them. This is almost common sense, but most of us don't take the time to reflect on the past day.

One way to do this is start with we are calling the energizer assessment report. This is a week-long reporting project where you are going to track the activities that you do day to day. It's something that you can do every 1-2 months to stay aware of what it is that drives you. This assessment report is a way to visually see what gives you energy and joy at work.

Here is how it works:

For each day this week that you work, write down the activity you do. When you move onto the next activity write down what it is. Next to each activity right down your energy level. To keep it simple we will use a 3-point scale.
1= Draining, grinding, exhausting
2= Moderate, no change, going through the motions
3= Exciting, engaged, enjoyable, energizing.

This exercise is designed to do one thing, create awareness. Ideally you will find at least one work activity that you do every day that you can mark as a 3. The other aspect of this exercise is to clearly see what types of activities regularly drain us.

The activities that drain us often affect how well we can work on tasks that proceed it. Here's an example. Let's say you really hate responding to customer emails, but your role entails that you do this at least a couple of times a day. What if every single day you start with the part of the job you hate the most. What tends to happen is that we lose energy, motivation, and momentum. By starting with the activities that we least like to perform we set ourselves up for being less effective on tasks we may enjoy a bit more.

After charting your energy levels and activities for a week or two try to look for recognizable patterns. Are all of your three's in the afternoon? Perhaps there is something to the timing of the day as well. Depending on your individual characteristics certain times of the day might be best for certain activities.

To share, I am a morning person. I wake up and feel really good, active, confident, etc. This is the time that I've learned to plan activities where sharp alertness is required such as data presentations or team meetings. In the afternoons, I don't have the same energy so if a task takes a lot of effort its best if I can get it done in the morning. The afternoons I save for preparations and putting together presentations for the next day.

This activity will help you gain insight to your unique working style. If you are going to work anyway mine as well figure out how you can do it a way that makes you effective and happy

Question Three: How can I challenge myself to grow?

The next step in our journey of deeper self-assessment is going to be most challenging one yet. The steps we've covered so far focus on about making sure that we are in the right place, and doing the right job. What happens when we feel that are in the right place and in the right role? How do we avoid complacency, more importantly how do we continue to grow? When we find ourselves in a good place it makes sense to push the boundaries. Naturally, the next step in our journey is figuring out how we can improve and gain the skills that gives us the confidence to lead. Along the way we are going to learn how to push beyond the norms while avoiding complacency.

There will always be motivation killers that pop up at various points in our lives. At work, motivation can come to a complete halt when we experience boredom, burn-out, unfulfillment, or a lack of progress. When we experience this type of mental adversity it can cause us to re-evaluate everything. You may start to wonder if the grass is greener somewhere else, or if things would have been better if you made a different career choice. Even the most successful individuals have spent time doubting what they are doing. The difference however, is that they know when and how to make the right shifts to get re-inspired.

With the next couple of reflection questions, we are going to explore how to get past the boredom that can occur after years of routine. One of the ways we are going to do that is to find out how we can move beyond ourselves. We are going to ask questions that can help you as an individual progress in ways you never thought possible. The reason why is because when we can ask questions about how we can do better; we can fend off the burn out that sets in when we aren't experiencing progression.

At a certain point in our roles we develop enough skills and confidence to get by in our current roles with relative ease. We can call this competence. With a high level of competence, it becomes easy to cruise. Stress is low, pay is good, life is grand. After some time in a role the challenge becomes easier if we don't push ourselves. The initial learning curve we had to climb has been conquered and our skill level starts to match the requirements of the job. What we don't want to happen is to become so complacent that we are no longer progressing. Instead we want to figure out how we can continue to grow and experience the same learning returns we did when we first started.

There is an assumption that individuals who read self-help books are the types of people that want more out of life. I'm not going to make that assumption, but I would venture to guess that you the reader may wonder what is missing from your career. As we've shared so far, it's our intention to set questions to guide you dig deeper and find your own answers. The content of this chapter is to help you reach the next level in your specific career. These questions are designed to help you discover a new challenge to work toward that you are both passionate and excited about. Challenges are where growth comes from and those who seek challenges deliberately will grow deliberately. These questions will guide you to discovering something new about yourself.

Guiding Questions on Challenging ourselves to Grow

Who motivates you, who inspires you?

Before we investigate this question further, we need to distinguish the difference between inspiration and motivation. These two words have similar purposes, they are adjectives we seek out to help us take action in some way. They are opposites in the sense that one pulls us forward, while the other pushes us from behind.

To be motivated means that you have found something outside of you that you want to work towards. Motivation is like the desert oasis that shows up when you are dying of thirst. With a hopeful future in front of you, you can dig deep and keep moving forward despite being on your last leg. In your own life you can find motivation by knowing what it is you want to achieve or have. These are outside factors that keep you taking action in some way.

Inspiration is that internal fire that makes us want to do great things. We are all able to conjure up inspiration when we set the right frame for ourselves. Being inspired means that there is something inside of us that compels us to take action. In a sense, inspiration can last a life time while motivation is a temporary burst of acceleration. When we see greatness in others it can spark the feeling of greatness within ourselves.

These concepts are important because we can use both to reach new levels of our potential. Think about the people around you who are always receiving praise. How good would it feel if you were able to receive some of the same recognition? What about the person on your team that is always hitting their numbers? Is there somebody on your team that you can benchmark as the hardest worker? Look for that person to find the motivation to do what's difficult. Motivation is what we can use to overcome difficult challenges.

Think about someone you admire or highly respect in your organization. What is it about them that you admire? There could be a number of factors that draws you to a person in this way. It could be that the person that you look up to is in a higher position and seem to do a good job at it. Maybe, it's the fact that they are close to your age but seem to really be progressing. Or maybe it's something that seems deeper than that such as their approach to work. You find inspiration by the way somebody approaches their work. Whatever it is, if you can start to identify the person or people you are inspired by you can start to identify the gaps that need to be fulfilled for you to get there.

Frame it like this. Right now, you are creating the person you want to be 1,2,5, or 10 years from now. To do this you should be identifying the qualities you want to possess. This is what makes you a unique and competent individual. This method works well because it's hard to know what we need before we have it. By looking up and ahead to individuals that we want to be like, we can start to work to adapt some of their admirable traits as our own.

Here are some other ways to answer this question. Look at the how the people you respect interacts with others. Do they talk with a certain presence? Are they particularly good at listening? It should matter how these individuals treat other people. The most effective leaders are in the position they are in because they know how to inspire beyond the job. They know how to dive deep and get the most out of there people.

When you ask this question and answer it for yourself try to create a list of the traits and qualities that this person has that you would like to possess. Also, take the time to identify any specific skills that these people have that you do not.

Finally, what is this person's approach to work? Do they seem to constantly be learning new things or innovating? While this may not be obvious on the surface it will give you a challenge to create a relationship with the people you are inspired by. If you can successfully get on their radar and spend time with them, you could learn how they approach there day to day. Absorption is what we are after.

In Summary:
Find someone who motivates you
Find someone who you can become inspired by
Identify the traits that you want to adapt as your own
Become someone who your former self would look up too.

How can you become above average?

Out of all of the questions in this book, this is the one can be the most challenging to answer. Why is it so hard to figure out how we can become above average? It's because many of us are already busting on our ass to do our best. How much more can we give!?

Going above average really means going beyond what you think is possible. This isn't a motivational book; this is a career guide that prompts deeper self-reflection in individuals. However, this question asks for something more. It asks you the reader to create possibilities that don't currently exist.

To go above average into the realm of greatness we need to go beyond the current version of ourselves. How we do that is by imagining without limits. In the words of Nelson Mandela "It always seems impossible until it's done." There was once a time that cavemen didn't know anything beyond the cave until someone asked, could we do this better? As soon as the question is asked the possibility becomes real.

So look around, look at your life, look at what you currently do and ask the question. Could I do this better? Is there a way that I could excel way beyond my current level? These are the types of reflection questions that will help you to uncover the answers to go beyond yourself.

The other part to this is the creating belief that its possible. You must believe that you are capable of more. Whether its affirmations, journaling, consistency, or self-hypnosis you have to start convincing yourself that there is more for you to give and have. Doubt can still pop up, but what we should strive for is to take action despite of the doubt/negative self-talk. Start training yourself to think big to grow. To put it practically, let's play around with some of our current belief states and see where we can make small shifts.

The fear of failure. It makes sense to put these words in this section because this is often what stops us from thinking bigger. We get scared that we can't accomplish what we set out to do. Setting bigger goals is scary and it's not unusual for our inner monologue to talk us out of attempting anything too far outside of our comfort zone. If we let ourselves listen to the repetitive "that's too hard or you can't do it" we will talk ourselves out of trying.

"If your thoughts are as tall as the height of your ceiling, you can't fly above your room."
—Israelmore Ayivor,

Thinking bigger and setting bigger goals is a skillset in its self. Partly this means giving yourself permission to think bigger. The other requirement is to start believing that anything you set your mind to is possible. Not in a corny way, but in a way where those words actually mean something to you. Your goal should be to able to tell somebody what your big goals are and believe that it's entirely possible for you to accomplish.

In the beginning of 2019, I set out to write and publish a book that I could be proud of. I set this goal never having done so before. For me to be proud of the book I was writing, it had to be a respectful length of quality content without fluffy rambles. I set this goal on Jan 1st, 2019 and told myself that I wanted to accomplish it. I can't tell you how many times that I doubted my self during the process. There would be multiple days where I would set up to write, coffee in hand, and nothing would happen. While discouraging, I kept repeating that phrase/quote/mantra that everything we see before us today was once considered impossible. It was enough to keep me going, keep me pushing through. The result of that push was 1) A finished book that I was proud of and 2) A growth of character that came from pushing myself to do something new.

It is the size of the challenges we intentionally set for us give us an opportunity to grow and rise above the level we are currently at.

In today's modern world we have so much comfort that our mind needs to create problems. You see it is the mind's job to solve problems, when life is good and there is no danger it looks elsewhere to create a problem. This is where the feeling of lack can come from. What happens is our safe, well fed, and comfortable selves look to create problems to solve. If not careful the problems that we create are the ones of comparison, materialism, and a need for validation. We feel that we are not good enough because of some external lack.

Instead what we could do is create challenges for ourselves that would be beneficial to solve. This is where these questions come from. Questions like how can I be above average in my performance? With a specific focus on challenges that are going to help us grow, we become better people. We can reach a higher potential in this way.

Ask yourself "What can I do to become above average?". Then set out to uncover answers, and/or more questions that will lead you to become stronger in some way. At the end of this section there will be a practice you can implement to dive deeper into this question.

When we look at what's average, we are seeing where the majority of individuals end up. Going back to math class for a second, imagine the bell curve. The bell curve looks something like this:

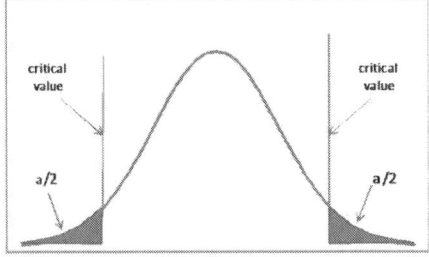

Most of the population in any one area groups in the center of the graph. Millions of people end up in the average category. In theory there is nothing wrong with that, but as someone who is striving for more it doesn't feel good to be called 'average'. If you are someone that is constantly working to improve or "figure it out", knowing that your efforts haven't moved you to the high tiers of the curve can be discouraging. Part of discouragement comes from a self-generated perception. However, a simple shift in focus can turn that dissatisfaction into encouragement.

One of the keys to unlocking an answer here is to better understand what we as individuals' value rather than what we think others want us to value. This creates a different measuring stick. Instead of playing in a game that you were forced into, you can figure out your own game to play. What we should look to do is find something that we love and create a success metric around that.

Look at your job and go back to reflect on the questions we previously answered around energy. Remember, which tasks are the ones that you get the most excitement and enthusiasm from. These are the areas where you can focus your growth on because these are also areas in which you have an authentic connection too. All we are doing here is finding a new way to measure. By reframing it in this way, we make powerful decisions on where we to direct our efforts. Our goal with becoming 'above average' is to not only find an area that we can excel at but also would want to excel at.

The concept of making this more about us makes the whole striving mentality easier to bolster. To be better than average, we have to find what we enjoy more than average. This goes back to some of the questions we asked earlier in the text. To really go beyond ourselves it's going to take a focus on areas that we would truly enjoy being above average at.

After you've found some clarity in this area the next part is to work on execution. To do this begin taking consistent action while constantly reminding yourself of the whys behind your effort. Remembering and reminding yourself why this is so important to you is the absolute key to sustained effort. This can be done by simply journaling on it in the mornings, reflecting nightly, or creating a routine around goal evaluation. This is what it takes. It takes this discipline because you need to start to believe in your own potential to overcome the obstacles that will inevitably get in your way.

What do you struggle with?

Let's get deep and address the concept of struggle. Struggle are the areas of work or life that always seem to stop us in some way. They could be specific tasks or areas of our personality that conflict with the responsibilities that we have. In the next couple of paragraphs, we are going to work through how to find the root cause of our problem areas. Then we can figure out what we can do to minimize these weaknesses.

We humans are complex, unique, and interesting individuals. We live in a world that has evolved so much that our evolutionary survival instincts don't serve us in a way as they once did. Where we used to have to worry about predators and things chasing us, now those real survival instincts are fears that no longer assist us. Despite living in a time of relative abundance many of us still feel the weight of anxiety, stress, and comparisons. Our brains are filled with noise that isn't always helpful.

What types of fears do you have? More specifically what is it that you struggle with regularly. Are there areas of your life that you seem to always feel some sort of lack in? These are scary questions to ask. It is human nature for us to overcompensate for our flaws and perceived weaknesses. Instead of looking at the areas that we struggle with we generally avoid them by burying them deep, hoping we can fill the void with external achievements.

When we talk about struggles in this specific context, we want to see if we can uncover areas of our mindset that seem to be holding us back in some way. What is it that gives you anxiety at work? Do you have fears around not being liked, not being ready, underperforming, oversharing, or is it something else? Think about the past few weeks, can you recall days where you just felt off? How about a day or two where you just didn't enjoy life? Did you bother to ask why and uncover what it was that actually bothered you there?

One of the areas that was discussed in my first book The Happy Cog was finding patterns in your life by regularly reflecting. A great way to see this play out is to journal. By journaling with a stream of thought type of method, we can start see our feelings and re-occurring thoughts clearly laid in front of us on paper (or text). If you can form a habit of reflecting consistently you can see some of the thoughts materialize consistently. This gives you an opportunity to change some of that self-talk that is not serving you well.

The reason why dealing with our inner critic is so challenging is because there are so many thoughts, we have a day that addressing them directly is difficult. Take the time to put some of these thoughts down in front of you. Essentially, this type of practice lets you "see" any mental challenges that you may be facing. This type of writing lets you extract and pin point all that noise. And that noise is what is contributing to our inner personal challenges.

Why this may seem like a bit wishy washy it is highly effective for adjusting your thinking patterns to that of a more successful version of yourself. Imagine that you take the time to reflect on what is going inside of your head at the end of each day or the first thing in the morning. At the very least you will learn a bit about your regular streams of thought. The best thing that can happen is you discover how to regularly enrich the positive mental habits that help you to perform at your best.

What we are trying to do is address the self-sabotaging negative talk by looking it in the face. In the habits section we are going to add an element of mind reprogramming that will allow us to make the best of what we have.

Let's get some clarity on the areas of ourselves that need improvement. What is it that you hate doing? Are there tasks or parts of your role that suck the life out of you? That's where we are going to start. These energy sucking activities may not align with your ideal job, but they still exist. There are some people who love focusing in on deeply analytic reports and data, while others want to talk high level and conceptual. Which one are you?

The reason we need to address this area is because a significant weakness can hurt your career in the long run. While we don't need to turn our weaknesses into strengths, we could do our best to minimize their impact.

My example. When I started a new role, the thought pattern that kept re-occurring was that I was overwhelmed and under skilled. After a deeper dive I saw was that I was extremely bad at time management. I wouldn't get all the things that I needed to get done with in the day. I would work a full 9 hour day, not take a lunch, and leave the office feeling completely overwhelmed. Imagine busting yourself an entire day, not allowing down time, and then leaving feeling like you still have more to do. At first the weakness I was trying to address was a lack of competency in the new role. However, what I learned after asking myself this same question was that there was more to it. The real reason why I was struggling wasn't because I didn't know what I was doing, but because I would jump from task to task making little to no progress. This conclusion only came after asking myself what I struggled with. I knew what the problem area was but reflecting allowed me to get to the specific cause and make the change.

Sometimes when we are having trouble with a certain aspect of our jobs it's not the task itself, but an area that activity that we struggle with. While I thought my problem was lack of know-how, it turned out that I struggled with prioritization. I was so focused on getting everything done that I didn't take the time to understand what needed to be done. Knowing this allowed me to fix a specific area that plagued me.

Now take the time to discover your own patterns. Find out where you may be focused on the wrong the things by noting when you aren't feeling your best. With enough spotlight on this specific question, you will discover that there are areas that you can make significant adjustments on.

Actions and Habits: Challenge yourself to grow

The Habits and Actions section is to help you take actionable steps based on the reflections you've done in the previous sections. The "challenge yourself to grow" habits will be challenging, but completing them will help you become the person you need to be to reach your goals.

These steps along with a PDF with all of the chapters questions can be downloaded at PinegroveZen.com/tools

Growth Habit 1: Find and join a group that can level up your game

One of the most well recognized paths to reaching greater levels of achievement is to spend time with people that want more out of life. Get inspired by actively participating in activities that surround you with highly motivated people. While the benefits may be obvious, there still can be hesitation around actually taking action on this step.

If you have read anything on self-improvement it's inevitable that you've heard this heavily utilized quote attributed to Jim Rohn. In which he says "You're the average of the five people spend the most time with". Data shows that there are correlations to the people you end up surrounded by. For example, if one of your friend gains weight there is a percentage increase that you yourself will also experience weight gain. The hypothesis to this effect is that we normalize what we see around us.

(see: www.nejm.org/doi/full/10.1056/NEJMsa066082).

To get to actually level up your game, you actually have to do the work. Hopefully you have taken the time to reflect a bit on the questions asked and now you get to act on those findings.

Sometimes the hardest part of doing something new is starting. Here is the action step that you need to take. You need to find a local group where you can meet with people who are trying to better themselves. Once you find the group, contact them and sign up to attend their first meeting/meet up/outing. This is a little, but huge step forward that is going to give you a real piece of momentum that you can take with you.

Here are some ideas for groups that will surround you with high frequency people:
Toastmasters
Meet up groups
Networking events
Local Entrepreneurship groups
Volunteering

Find the time and go to one of these events regularly. Surrounding yourself with people who are actively trying to improve areas of their lives is going to keep you motivated to keep growing. The idea of encompassing yourself with a "better" peer group is that you subconsciously will normalize the actions that people are taking. In other words, by spending time with groups of people that are challenging themselves regularly you will consistently reach for growth over complacency. This influence is a natural effect that happens when your reference points are also striving for more.

If it feels a little bit uncomfortable it's definitely a step in the right direction. Discomfort is where growth comes from. Eventually the discomfort subsides and we've achieved a secondary skill of becoming a bit more courageous. Each time we do something that stretches us a bit, we expand our own comfort zones.

While the main benefit we are seeking here is growth by osmosis we can't neglect the opportunity to make new friends. Friends are just groups of people who find similarities with each other that they like. While actively working on your own skill sets, take the time to learn something new from people. At a minimum you get a to learn new skills set from challenges you take on and in a best case scenario you find a friend that becomes a new connection in your life.

Growth Habit 2: Find that one area where you can go beyond average.

Have you ever gone after something you truly love doing?

The way to go above average and become great is really easy if you know what to do. You simply need to know what you want to do. The way to know what you want to do is to pick out an area of your life or skill that you have that you enjoy doing.

Let's go back to the reflection questions, think about what types of skills or activities that give you the most energy. Once you have identified those specific areas, decide which one is going to get above average focus from you. Generally, we get what we put in. If we want to go above and beyond, we just need to find one thing to go above and beyond in then use that to create synergies with our other unique strengths.

Here are the steps to go beyond average in an area.
1) Find out what activities or tasks give you natural energy
2) Decide on one activity where you are going to commit a little bit more time
3) Schedule/Block off time to improve that specific skill regularly
4) Commit to improving over the next 90 days

Ok, ok easy enough right. Now, let's get a bit more granular on the skill itself. How can you actually take something that you are already doing well and go beyond it? What are the practical steps? You have a loose plan in place and have made a decision on what you want to work on. Being able to actually do that is another question in itself, one that we are going to address here so you can move forward and evolve.

The first thing you need to do after deciding is break down the skill or area itself. That way we can look how to refine and make it better.

1) Brainstorm the Elements - Write down all of the elements involved in the new 'thing' you are working on. For example, if I what I would like to become a better presenter I would write all of the mini skills associated with presenting. My list would look something like this...

Presenting – speaking, designing presentations, power point, projecting, presence, reading a room, engaging, flow, and much more.

Take some time to brainstorm all of the elements, that way you can address specific areas of leveling up without being overwhelmed.

2) Decide on which element to work on – Now what we can do is focus in on a specific area to improve. It's a good idea to focus on one part of the skill per week. That way you can focus on really improving and being well rounded. Using the presentation example from above, a 90 day schedule might look like something like this.

Week 1 – Focus on speaking with volume
Week 2 – Designing powerful slides
Week 3- Engaging an audience
Week 4 – Creating flow in presentations
Week 5 - Developing a presence
Week 6 – Working with a co-presenter

Week 7-12 – and so on

... Essentially what this habit is asking you to do is to discipline yourself to create a curriculum around something you want to get better at. This type of self-directed teaching helps us improve in several ways. First it challenges us to think deeper about the area that we would like to improve on. By breaking it down it to specific elements we understand all the nuances of how to be great at something. Secondly, by creating our own curriculum to follow we learn how to learn. This method allows us to teach ourselves which makes for more effective and stickier learning.

Question Four: What type of leader can I become?

Lead with purpose, lead with intent, and serve others.

Up until now our reflective focus has been about us as an individual. As we continue on our progression to reach higher levels of meaning, it makes sense to learn more about ourselves as leaders. After all, if we do the right things consistently it's inevitable that one day we will be asked to lead. With this new mantle of responsibility, new questions should be asked in order to be effective. Leading other people is a game changer as far as responsibility goes. Failing here can hurt other people. To prevent failure in this area we must again learn to be intentional about our actions.

Maybe, you don't want to be a leader. The idea of management doesn't resonate with you or maybe, being a part of leadership teams isn't your dream. There is nothing wrong with that. Many people can go on to be high level individual contributors while also finding joy, happiness, and financial success. Regardless, those who become consistently successful are deemed leaders even if not by their titles. Every team in an organization has a few super stars that others look up to. If you become someone that others look up to, wouldn't it make sense to understand how you can best help?

I believe one of the reasons why there is such an abundance of online courses, services, and self-help books today is because helping other people succeed feels so damn good. When you as an individual reach a place where you feel like you've "figured it out" you want to tell everyone. Sharing what you know so well feels natural. If you take the time to become a good leader you will be able to scale your message like you've never thought possible. There is something deeply fulfilling about being able to share a message that truly resonates with somebody else.

If you've ever had the pleasure of a colleague, peer, or friend tell you that your particular words helped them solve a big problem in their life then you know how that feels. This feeling of serving others beats most other rewards in the human experience. If you truly want to feel lifelong happiness and fulfillment consider becoming a leader in some way. First become the best version of yourself by figuring out how to handle your own personal challenges. After you have learned the lessons you needed to learn, share your knowledge with the world. Leave something tangible.

The guiding questions in this chapter are framed to help you really think about serving others in the best way. You don't have to be a loud charismatic and ultra-charming guy/girl to be a successful leader. No, what you need is to know your people. You need to know your gifts and who would benefit most from them. Most importantly you need to know how to connect.

Guiding Questions on How to lead

Who do you want to lead?

We have spent a lot of time reflecting on questions that focus on how we as individuals can continue to progress. It is vital that we take the time to understand ourselves so we can use those insights to become better leaders. In this section, the focal point shifts onto understanding how we can use our unique skills to help people in the most powerful way we can.

Before we really dive into the how to become a leader, we should first figure out who to lead. What this means is that we want to be able to get very clear about who we want to serve. Clarity in this area allows us to go after leadership in a way that benefits us while also benefitting those we are helping. What is ideal is if we can become someone that raises our level of responsibility without compromising the amount of enjoyment we get from our roles. Essentially, we are getting clear on what it would look like to have our cake and eat it too.

Start thinking about what you want as someone that gets identified as a leader. Imagine the types of responsibilities that you have. Perhaps more importantly, start thinking about the people that you will be leading.

A good way to start diving deeper into this question is to start first with those that you like. Who are the people in your organization that you genuinely like? Are they people on your team or are they friends from different business units? Are they hard working or are they cool laid back, but successful?

There is something magical that happens when teams working toward achieve a central goal also like, respect, and enjoy each other's company. When there is a positive emotional connection to others on the team, achieving great metrics becomes much more likely. Now, imagine that you are responsible for a group's success. If you actually care how people are doing beyond the metrics not only will you gain respect, but you will be able to lead more effectively. It may be obvious, but it becomes so much easier to win when there is a genuine connection amongst leaders and employees. Now imagine that you created a team of individuals that like you as well. Don't you think they are going to fight a little bit harder work toward the goals you set forth?

Another very important element in thinking about who it is that you want to lead is to think about the type of person that you want on your side when things aren't going well. Inevitably, at some point in your journey you will face adversity. When you are identified as a leader more pressure is put on you. Not everything always goes smoothly and it may not even be your fault, but it's the way it goes. The stronger the people around you are the better chance you have at using adversity as a learning tool. To be able to do that you must create a team of those individuals that have the ability to see challenges as opportunities for growth.

It's easy to assume that when you imagine yourself as a leader you conjure up leading a team of those less experienced then you. If you think about it, having a group of younger eager employees working for you is probably less intimidating then being surrounded by people that know what they are doing. After all, how are you going to add value to someone who has been doing a job twice as long as you? How would you handle that? If you've been in the workforce long enough you have probably witnessed what it's like when an unexperienced manager gets put into a position of 'power'. The veterans on that team don't respect them. Well, not at first. They have to earn it.

We are thinking through the types of individuals that you may end up leading so we can better identify what's ideal. What we can do with this information is create a picture of the type of people that you would like to create a team with. This allows you develop your own leadership style to align with who it is that you want to lead. When you are answering this question really take the time to imagine it. The imagination part is really a practice in clarity. The clearer you can make something the more likely you can incorporate it into reality.

Keep in mind you don't necessarily have to think about this in the context that you are thrown into a position with a team already in place. Instead you could look at this exercise as an opportunity to create your own team of like-minded individuals that you can collaborate with. These are the type of people that you would want to bring in to help you with your big idea.

I've found my best working relationships by identifying who I want to work with. It is almost like once you've identified the qualities you are looking for it becomes so much easier to find. The practice of getting certain on who you want to surround yourself with creates a guide on how to find those people.

Now you try, figure out the qualities of the people that you want to team up with. While you write the answers to this question out you will be surprised how easily you can picture specific individuals that you will want to connect with. Here is an example of how someone may answer this question:

I love working with people who have a passion about what they do. They may not love every single aspect of their job, but when asked what parts of this role do you love they have an answer. They are always asking themselves how they can exceed their own expectations and progress. I realize not everybody is like this and that's ok, but I find it much harder to collaborate with those individuals that have no desire for growth. They come in bitter about seemingly everything. Those are not the type of people that I want to bring in on my team

Instead I want to lead people that want to achieve. When I say achievement, I mean achievement in their own way. I know when I work with people who have a passion about something it's much easier to identify powerful strengths, they have that we can use on our current projects. I want to lead people who want to improve themselves and I don't care if it's for the specific business I am in. What I want to be able to give them is a place where they can find their strengths. Then take those strengths and find their own path. The ideal person that follows me is someone that is open to see if there is a better way, but also not afraid to try things out to make mistakes. I don't want someone completely obedient; I want to be challenged as a leader myself so I can grow and improve. Ideally, I am looking to assemble a team of individuals with their own super powers. It will be my job to find out what really drives them in order to get the most out of every member of my team.

What areas of the business do you want to grow?

What are you passionate about?
What do you enjoy doing?
What could you help nurture?

Long term success is going to be entirely dependent on our level of enjoyment. It is so important to enjoy what we do if we want to be good at what we do. When we bring some level of intention to the process of leadership, we can set a course to find our very own niche within the organization. The reflection question here asks us again to think about what it is that we want.

Here we should start thinking about what areas of the business align with our interests of growth. This is why having an initial self-awareness is so important. You should continue to be asking questions that help you to get more clarity on what does make you happy. Keep it top of mind as a priority to know yourself better than anyone else.

The reality of being awesome at your job is that doesn't work if you don't have a genuine interest in what you do. People talk about following their passion all the time because it's a truth that deep down we all know. Passion is the part of ourselves that lights up with excitement. It is the type of energy that allows us to feel alive when we tap into it. There are few parts of the human experience greater than being able to spend time working on something that genuinely lights us up.

What areas of the business do you want to grow? We ask this question as a point of advancement. When moving up the career ladder, the responsibilities, pay, and commitment needed all increase. It's vital that if you are thinking about moving up within your company or organization that you take the time to know where it is you want go. You must think about what you want to do. Try to identify those moments that you get a bit more excited for then others.

A unique way to tackle this question is to look at it from where you find yourself feeling the most frustration. Can you recall or identify moments at work where you adamantly disagree with decisions that leadership is making? Do you rant and rave about the 'mis-steps' your organization is making? Think about the last time you were so confident that leadership was making an incorrect decision. If you can then it means you are tapped into some kind of interest. If you really didn't care then there would be no reaction. However, showing strong emotions or convictions is a sign that there is a certain energy available for you to tap into. Lean in there. Let yourself feel the passion that is expressed as anger. This is your authentic self, letting you know that you have something worth exploring.

We can start with the areas where we exhibit emotions and then work are way up. Work is hard sometimes, but the solution is to find the parts of it that connect with you in a meaningful way. It's the same message we've been talking about, but now applied to becoming a leader. Where is it that you can find meaning and how can you actively work toward making that meaning impactful?

The question at hand is **"What area of the business do you want to grow?"**.

Let's imagine a scenario where you are a gardener in a giant lot. This is your job now. You now work on this giant lot. There is a huge variety of plants, flowers, and vegetables that can all be grown in this fertile soil. When you first got hired at the garden company you were assigned to make sure all of the crops are watered an adequate amount every day. You take a lot of pride in what you do here. You've been exceptionally organized and understand the importance of making sure that you are doing your part.

After you have proven yourself as an exceptional waterer, the lead gardeners tell you that you are get to be in charge of your own area in the lot. Finally, your big promotion!

You now have this choice. Before you there are acres of well-nourished land and you get to decide which part of this beautifully synergistic space is your new responsibility. You look around, there is so much that you like. You know from experience that you could become a waterer manager. These are the people in charge of the waterers, they make sure that the water is clean and constantly flowing into the waterer's buckets. In the distance you see the designers, these are the people that get to decide what goes where. There is lots of planning involved in this one. Even further back there is a group of people who research the next crop they want to produce. Because you've been such a good waterer you have options of where to go. You ask yourself what do I want to nurture? What do I want to help grow?

Remember these analogies as you move up your career. Your best shot at succeeding as a leader is to have a desire to improve a certain area of the organization. It can be hard to know what you want to do if you have been siloed in a certain area for a long time. Whenever you start to feel that familiar feeling of boredom, try to step back from your current position to look at the bigger picture. Maybe, there are opportunities within the organization that you never even considered. Allow yourself to think beyond what you know how to do and instead start picturing what you would want to do.

Part of moving up in a company while also enjoying it is being very authentic with the decisions you make. This includes moving up into leadership positions. Remember, we aren't simply trying to game system by moving up the ladder in way that ends up feeling empty. The questions being asked are all designed to get to the root of what we want. Ask it, but allow yourself to dig deep for the answers.

Make everything about you and what you want. Let yourself be happy where you are.

What kind of leader do you want to be?

A mentor, a coach, an inspiration, a motivator, a friend....

The type of leader that you will ultimately become entirely depends on how you personally define leadership. If you never take the time to create your own definition of a leader, someone else will define it for you. For this to be fulfilling you have to ask yourself the questions that will force you to be really intentional with how you serve others. What's so beautiful about this is that when you define who you want to become, you start creating a path for you to reach that ideal.

Don't limit yourself to what you know now. Instead ask this question and allow yourself to aspire to what is may not yet be possible. To be clear: Ask, then think big.

Your growth as a leader is going to depend on how clearly you know what kind of leader you want to be. There are many individuals out there who have chased and captured the title of what they think is a leader. Titles like manager/boss/supervisor/director don't necessarily make you a leader. What makes you a leader is being worthy of being followed. When you feel like you need advice or direction in your life, is there a certain person that you tend to reach out to? What are the traits of that individual?

As you start to reflect on who you define as a leader, start to create the ideal image of yourself as leader. How are you showing up every day? Do you have an attitude that is forward moving?

Most of all do you have a good attitude toward what you do or is this just a means to an end. The way to be a role model that people look up to is to generate the qualities of a person worthy of being followed. To get to the point where others are intentionally seeking you out, you need to start doing the things where other people would want to seek you out. You have to become more then you are right now. This should feel challenging, if you are asking these questions in the right way the answers should stretch you further then where you currently are. To lead is to continue to grow, you can't be content with where you at. If you are ok with being the same skill level you are now how can you expect to motivate others toward excellence.

A great leader is able to naturally inspire people to reach their highest potential. The best bosses are the ones that are operating in a way where others want to go beyond themselves. It goes back to the idea of frequencies. To succeed in a leadership position, you yourself must consistently operate in a high vibrating frequency. When the people that follow you are around your high-level frequency and energy, naturally they will move upward.

The way I define leadership is somebody that is sought out because of the value that they provide to those want to grow. To do this well, you need to constantly and consistently being looking to grow yourself.

Let's get back to the question, **what kind of leader do you want to be?**

Really allow yourself to define exactly what this will look like. The best way to do this is to conjure up as many positive traits that you would associate with someone you would want to work for. Bring all of these qualities to the surface so you have some pieces to work with. Then create an avatar for your ideal boss.

When you are answering this question take the time to describe the idealness of the leader you want to be. To give you an idea, here is how I have answered the question in the past:

The type of leader that I want to be is someone that leads by example. I want people to follow me based on what I do rather than listen to me simply because they have to. To be that type of leader I know that I need to become someone more than I am now. The kind of leader that I want to be is someone that sees the potential in people and knows how to get them to work toward it. I picture myself being able to recognize someone who is pushing themselves to be great and to encourage and recognize that quality in them.

What I want to bring to my conversations is a realness and understanding that work can be a struggle sometimes. I believe that I can help those that are struggling find a way to enjoy what they do while they do it more. My style is one of that inspires my employees to work hard because they see that I am doing everything I can to better serve them. I believe I have great ideas, but my ideas will be vetted with those on my team because we are in this together. A good leader gets feedback and learns from his mistakes.

As a leader to others it's my job to 'get the most of my people'. I do that by recognizing that they are people and treat them as such. I've been in a position in the past where I felt that the only thing that mattered about me was hitting my numbers. I want to make sure that I never forget how that felt so that when I lead people, I can make them feel their individuality. I encourage uniqueness and new different ideas. I ask people what they are thinking, I give them credit and I help them to become leaders themselves. All of this allows me to stay driven to become better each and every day. I know that when I am able to spark passion and joy inside others I myself become motivated to become a better leader.

Finally, as a leader I aspire to be someone that continues to grow. Someone that continues to set new goals. I see myself as a role model who is consistently working on how to become a better version of myself, while also staying connected to what's important. It's not all about work, it's also about life. I want to lead a balanced life. One that is full of enjoyment with loved ones. A life where I rest. Friends and genuine connections. To be able to have this life while also moving a group of people forward is what I am moving toward.

I remember asking myself this question and not being sure of how I would answer at first. Remember, the answers can come at any time. The important thing is to just keep asking the question. As you gain insights and new experiences the right answers will come. For now, ask the question and answer it as authentically and fulfilling as you possibly can in this moment.

Actions and Habits: Leadership

The Habits and Actions section is to help you take actionable steps based on the reflections you've done in the previous sections. The "Leadership" habits are all about being intentional. By completing these activities, you will start thinking about leading and how you can help others.

These steps along with a PDF with all of the chapter's questions can be downloaded at PinegroveZen.com/tools

Leadership Habit 1: Learn how to connect

You may want to be a leader and you may also be taking all the right steps to become one, however, things don't always happen on our timelines. There is an element of patience that is required when trying to reach the next position in your company. You should not let the timing stop you from starting to cultivate and grow your leadership skills. One way to start that process of growth is to find someone to mentor.

You don't have to call even have to call it mentorship if that happens to provoke something rigid in you.

The task we are taking on here is to first think of someone who you could help. It could be someone on your team that you have more experience then. Maybe, there is an individual in the company that reminds you of yourself at an earlier point in the career. Practice some subtly here. Invite your colleague for a sit down or lunch without the intention of becoming their mentor.

Ideally you want to be able to connect with this person outside of the office. People tend to open up more when you get outside of work.

The challenge here is to become the type of person that people do open up to. To become a leader in the eyes of others, you will need to be the type of person that others naturally seek out for advice.

Here is how to do that:

You yourself must be able to get those around you to ask themselves good questions. Most people don't like being told what to do. Which is why if you can create and ask good questions of other people you will notice how they can open up. There is no big secret to asking the right question, but there is a method to get someone to dive deeper. You must listen fully. Developing a skill of active listening is helpful. This means listening in a way where you absorb what someone else is saying, rather than listening to respond.

To Summarize:

1) Ask good questions
2) Actively Listen
3) Find out where their natural enthusiasm is
4) Dive deeper
5) Share
6) Repeat.

It might look something like this. You take a colleague out to lunch, knowing that this is someone you want to help with. Maybe, its somebody that you see a younger version of yourself in. Or someone facing similar challenges.

When you get a chance to sit down and talk with someone, use the opportunity to learn more about them. Remember ask good questions. A good question here has three elements 1) It is interesting for the other person to answer 2) It is open ended 3) Has the possibility of creating insight. Think of it this way, if you are able to ask someone a question that leads them to create lifelong personal insight, they will appreciate you more than you know.

Be interested in what they have to say. Listen as intently as you can. When you listen this way, you will be able to hear notes that resonate. To clarify: there are moments in conversations where an individual's authentic interest is brought to the surface. As a good listener you will be able to stretch those moments out and expand upon them. Not only does this lead to better conversations, it creates real connection. As a future leader being able to connect is a skill that must be developed.

Leadership Habit 2: Create an inspiring conceptual guide for your current role

Teaching is the best way to learn.

This chapter's question has been all about leadership. How to define it, how to become it, who to lead, and so on. One of the essential elements of a good leader is the ability to teach others and help them grow. Sometimes high achieving individuals aren't necessarily the best teachers because their excellence is something they may not think about intentionally. Think about that sales superstar or master programmer in your company. They may be the best at what they do but would you also give them the title of the best trainer?

It's not always the case, but the reason why so many successful doers aren't necessarily the best teachers is because they haven't taken the time to learn the skill. Why would they, right? A person that is successful in their field or role understandably has an extremely focused view on how to move forward with their goals.

If you are somebody that is a high performer, I am going to encourage you to learn how to teach. The way we are going to do this is by extracting what you know at a high level. The habit/practice we are going to implement is to create a guide for your current role. The challenge here is to create a document no more than two pages in length that can teach someone the most important aspects of your job. What is so effective about this is that it forces you to think high level about what is that you every day.

Imagine that you get promoted and the only thing you can leave behind to train the next person is this guide you create. You must really think about it is that is most important. The biggest challenge is to create the guide in a way that's going to make the most impact to the person reading it.

Here is how you could put this into motion: Answer the following prompts with a paragraph or two. Find a time when you can sit down with a cup of coffee and work through this. You might be surprised with what you come up with.

Concept: What is this role's function? What is the big picture?

Mindset: What mindset should someone take in this role if they want to be successful?

What does it take to become an Elite Performer in this position?

What challenges could a new person expect? What are challenges that I myself had to learn?

What are the most valuable skills to learn? What skills are essential

Validations/Rewards? What types of rewards are available to me in this role?

To help you see this habit flushed out, I had written out some responses to a past role. Putting this habit into practice forces you to think about what it is that you do every day. Overtime your concepts, ideas, and thoughts about the position may evolve to become even more powerful

Concept: *As a Key Account Manager, It is my job to be a partner to our customers in the NW United States. The big picture is to build solid trusted relationships with the contacts of the customers I work with every day. The way I do that is by using the tools, insights, and knowledge I gain and share it in a way with my customers that is highly actionable. I must know what tools we have available for our customers and at a high level be able to recommend these tools to be integrated with their processes. It is my job to help my customers meet the goals they set for themselves, it is also my job to help them come up with achievable goals.*

Mindset: *Strive for excellence. Impress through effort and consistency. Provide consistent and authentic value. The way I want my customers and my team to feel about me is that we are all moving in a forward direction together. Every day I show up and I ask how can connect with my customers in a way that gives them something they don't have.*

What it takes for Elite Performance: *To be elite in this role you have to constantly ask the question, how can I be an above average performer in this role? You have to ask yourself this question so you can create answers and gain insights. At first you may not know what it takes to be an elite performer, but over time you will understand what base level is then be able to rise above expectations. Keep the concept and desire to serve at a high level and you will be able to as you gain the knowledge and insights needed. Going above and beyond does require above and beyond effort. Every day you must be intentional with the actions that you take. Create a curriculum of on-going learning and figure out areas where you can become an expert in.*

Challenges to expect: *With great ambition comes an abundance of possible activities that can be done. This is a role that has the freedom to decide what the next best step is. However, a newer account manager can be overwhelmed by what to do next. The biggest challenge that you will face as a new account manager is knowing how, and what to focus on. The advice that I will share is to learn how to prioritize. It will take a bit of time to know what is important, but knowing that prioritization is needed will save you a lot of time and effort. Also, not everything is all roses. Sometime things suck and when that happens you have to dig deep to find meaning. When you are having a rough day, take some time to step back and reframe the challenges.*

Skills to Learn: *This is an ongoing process. A key account manager is a complex role with many moving parts and intricacies. There is this constant growth opportunity to learn how to be a more effective communicator while also becoming a knowledge expert. It's not always easy to manage your time, but having a good understanding of the type of AM you want to be will help tremendously. One of the most valuable skills will be your ability to network. Learn to find out who does what and build a relationship with those liaisons.*

Validations/Rewards: *Everyone has a different idea of what types of rewards they wish to seek. Some people on our team are motivated by the financial rewards, others feel good when they solve problems, or get recognized by leadership. There are tons of variables as too what makes you feel good about what you do. To really have success and continued motivation one good question to ask yourself if what rewards fulfill me? For me personally in this role, I found my spirits listed when I was able to share a concept or an idea with the rest of the team that resonated. I had the opportunity to share ideas often and when what I had to say resonated with others on my team, they let me know. That felt really good and encouraged me to share my ideas often. This type of validation inspired me to get better at my role and find out which parts of the job I really enjoy*

What all of this does.
Putting this habit into practice makes you get really good at your job. After being in a role for some time you naturally adapt to it and get better with it. This task requires you to reconnect to learning. Now you get to look at what you do day to day from a high level so that it can be broken down and taught. This is hard because it requires you to think about what you do instead of showing up and doing it.

The fun part of this is that the activity itself creates new insights into what you do. You will notice that after you create this conceptual guide that you may find more drive and fulfillment in your role.

Question Five: Where can I create synergy?

1+1= 3

Being able to lead is one thing, but to reach the highest level one thing you will need is to start thinking about areas of synergy. There are parts that don't yet exist within your organization where teams could start to work together. Can you come up with good ideas that bring more collaboration? The next part of leveling up involves starting to think about the bigger picture. You need to start to ask questions that you may have never even brought to the surface.

Throughout this chapter we are going to work to discover deeper insights about how we can help our organization excel. Our goal is to create opportunities that have yet to be uncovered while also organically building a network.

Here is a thought experiment. Imagine that in your everyday role you are approached by a high-ranking executive within your organization, it could be the CEO a COO or another title. This individual who you highly respect approaches you and says that he/she wants to know what it is that makes your team successful. He asks you to lists the best practices of the individuals in your role. He tells you that he is looking for the efficiencies. What is it that your team does well? After speaking with you the CEO tells you that he learned a lot. You were able to provide him with a level of detail that fired him up as well as impressed him with your thought process.

You see that he has a sheet in front of him with your team name. All of the insights you shared were written down with the most impactful ones circled in green. The executive goes then off to the next team and repeats the process. What he is doing is making connections. He is finding out where teams can better work together. Successful companies that grow are able to do so in a way that they operate more fluently.

The challenging part though is how do you do this in a way that it's not just piling on more work with people. Making connections across company roles is easy enough, but to implement practices that create efficiencies takes some real focus.

The questions we are going to ask in this section focuses on extracting the knowledge you may already have in this area. To ask the right question is to get the right answer. Also, asking these questions will bring a higher-level awareness to the workings of the corporate machine you may be in.

Guiding Questions on Creating Synergy

Where does cohesion already exist?

What parts of the company are already working together, can any of those processes be improved?

Most of us are so involved in our day to day we never even get a chance to think about how to improve processes. After all there are specific executives hired for just this sort of thing. After years of growing an organization these executives can lose sight of the things that you may be able to see closer to the front lines. The questions in this section are going to prompt us to think past our roles as contributors and create awareness around operational efficiencies. One of the benefits to this type of thought experiment is that it makes you that much more valuable.

Allow yourself to think bigger in your role as often as possible. Not only will you be stretched beyond your current beliefs, but you will discover that by asking these questions you are becoming a strategic high-level thinker.

Sometimes the insights you have aren't that strong. You may come up with ideas that just aren't practical. They might not resonate with anyone but yourself. Don't get discouraged keep asking and keep learning how to be a creator of ideas and a creator of questions. On other occasions you may pull out a gold nugget that can vastly improve the organization. If you discover one of these gems, refine it, and share it as much as you possibly can. The only way to truly vet a good idea is to get the feedback by putting it out there.

It can be a bit challenging to think about your organization in this way. Often its helpful to reframe our questions or break them down in ways that we can come up with answers. This is a good way to gain more perspective as we dive deeper into these insights. Using the examples below, try to see how you might answer each question. Write them down and keep them top of mind with the intention of sharing when opportune.

1) What individuals do I regularly work with that aren't a part of my department? And could our interactions be impactful at scale?

Example: I regularly interact with a team that brings in new 'suppliers. All of the individuals on my team have to interact with the 'new supplier team'. It is a vital part of the role we are in; however, the actual process can be time consuming and there are several hands involved. Cohesion could exist if we could create a process that involves fewer individuals for a more streamlined approach. More discussions need to happen around this, I can arrange a meeting with my contact to discuss an approach.

2) What have I done in my past that could be used to create efficiencies in my current role? If you have helpful experiences from your past, bring it to the surface.

Example: In my past role I worked to bring in new customers. I had little understanding of what could actually be accomplished by connecting more with the people on the set-up process. How much more effective could our new sales teams be if they really understood what we were capable of post-sale? On the other side, Account Managers could better understand what 'sold' the customer in the first place by having a kick off meeting with new sales people. This could help them start of the relationship by focusing in on what the customer believes he or she is getting.

When you start really thinking about all the roles that people have within your company you can feel a bit overwhelmed with these questions. After all, how can one individual not in a high leadership position make or even suggest changes at this level? It's fair to think that. However, this is a thought experiment to push yourself to become the type of person that can make the changes. Sure, you may not be in the position where you can snap your fingers and make something happen. But imagine, if you are one of the few people that actively asks this question you can and will come up with the type of answers that stretch you.

Challenge yourself to think about the big picture as often as you can. When you face a particular challenging part within your role or with your customers, think about what job functions you need to have to make your process easier. We ask questions we haven't asked before to get answers we haven't thought of before. If you've ever experienced burn out at work, you know what happens when we get too complacent. Having challenges that encourage us to think beyond ourselves is a good way to stay engaged and continue learning.

Actions and Habits: Synergy

The Habits and Actions section is to help you take actionable steps based on the reflections you've done in the previous sections. The "Synergy" actions in this section prompt you to make real progress. By completing the challenges below you will be able to create connections within your organization while organically growing your network.

These steps along with a PDF with all of the chapter's questions can be downloaded at PinegroveZen.com/tools

Creating Synergy Habit 1: Project Challenge

Have you ever felt frustrated that about the amount of work you put in without seeing any reward? Humans are complex creatures. Inside all of our own heads is a massive highway of neural networks. These networks are filled with thoughts, feelings, and things we have to do. Most people feel that they are constantly busy and working harder than everyone else. All this gives us the feeling that our efforts mostly go unnoticed.

A way past all of this is to be able to lead a project that pulls people together. If you can successfully create a team that singly focuses on the mission you put before them, others will take notice. This is one of the best ways to stick out. Of course, it takes some effort, creativity and you still might fall but putting the effort in will be worth the lessons you learn.

The way to really make a name for yourself and start getting on the short list of the positions you desire is to take initiative. The word initiative means "the power or opportunity to act or take charge before others do". The beautiful thing about the opportunity to create something new is that its available to everyone, but only those willing are the ones able to grab the spot.

The Project Challenge: is a straight forward idea where you push yourself to take a big step forward. Here is what you are going to do. With courage you are going to come up with an idea that benefits more than just yourself and then get a coalition together to complete the mission.

While the words in front of you can help you take a step. Real growth is going to come from the doing on this one. If you are ready for this step it will take some work and several skills in order to 1) Come up with a project idea 2) Pitch the project to a team you form 3) Execute 4) Pitch to a larger group. At the very least you demonstrate leader skills and a willingness go above and beyond the task at hand. For most this challenge is also a significant stretch of the comfort zone.

To help brainstorm some ideas for your project, consider some of the prompts below. Start generating ideas in areas where you feel a connection too, then figure out who you can collaborate with.

Where in the organization do, I think I can make a difference? (First List several Areas)
-New Sales (because of perspective)
-Data Analysis with real context
-Within this team, extracting strengths
-Overcoming Challenges Presentations
-Idea Generation (regular sessions)

Elaborate further on the list above (Few Ideas)

New Sales- I believe that I could make a difference here because of my background and new learned perspectives in the current role. I know what it's like to sell to prospects who aren't completely sold on the value proposition. I could work with new sales teams individually and tailor a 1-time presentation that gives additional perspective and ideas of how this could be executed.

Data Analysis with Real Context- Working closely with a really in-it data team member we could create a webinar of our findings that adds expertise and credibility to our organization, especially around data. We could take our findings and share it in a report with context from multiple positions and maybe use a few of our team members to work with us in a big and meaningful way.

Within the team, extracting strengths – Profile each member of the team and include their support people and a manager to get a full scope of what you think the best qualities and strengths of each team member are. Create a resource of who to go to for what becoming a highly effective team.

Overcoming Challenges Presentations – Create a class or series of presentations about how to create effective presentations with your audiences. Get real partners to participate with our team to present these in a meaningful way. Create a series/workshop about how to give good presentations.

Idea Generation Session- Start up and run an idea generation group where several team members gather together from different teams to brainstorm topics that might one day become a real actionable item. The idea generation leader would need to come up with a prompt and promote positive conversation. It would be a challenging but fun session to run.

Who, what team members would you like on each project?

New Sales – New sales project where people selling new collaborate more with people who are working the accounts every day. A one-time presentation ... Members needed: 1) New sales team member 1 or 2 2) Myself and/or another Account Manger 3) Training team member or Marketing to help create the deck and then promote it. 4) A champion customer.

Data Analysis with Real Context- Deep dive data project where we work with 1-2 top data members, 1-2 Account Managers, A training member for set up and deliver a powerful presentation around the stories that data is telling us

Within the team, extracting strengths – Because the goal of this project is to extract a strength profile of individuals there would need to be time allocated to sit down with team members. The discussions could be summarized by myself and one management team as well as coordinating with other teams.

Overcoming Challenges Presentations – Myself, Manager, An internal 'best presenter', marketing insights person.

Idea Generation Session- A generation session with a motivated set from several teams. Some ideas 1-2 members from Account Management, Accounting, User Experience, Development, etc. Each session could have a different prompt and several members from that group.

Result you want - *Take all of the ideas that you've come up with and in a couple of sentences write what the results you want are. This can really help you figure out how you can 'sell' the project to get others on board.*

Making a name for yourself beyond role requires exceeding expectations, and constantly proving you are someone that cares about what he/she does. Here is what happens to many—they work their asses off, they get some minor recognition but it fades and so does their ambition. A cycle that involves making concentrated efforts only to receive occasional bits of praise makes it really hard to stay committed. Instead be more strategic and thoughtful about the effort you make.

The way to make a difference in all that is by doing things that put you in front of more people. Use this guide to spark some of your own ideas and see if you can create something meaningful.

Question Six: How do I create lasting impact?

Finally, we are ready to take our last steps in this continued journey. This last section is going to ask us to think about the impact we make long after we are gone. So far, we've learned how to connect with the mission of an organization, develop personally, how to grow our skills, how to lead, and how to create connections. Now we are heading into an area that is easy in concept, but very difficult in execution.

The final step essentially requires us to become an entrepreneur within our organization. To do this we must learn how to take on a level of accountability as if it were all on the line. Reaching this feeling and level of responsibility puts power right back in our hands. It can give our days more meaning especially if we are able to fully embody the idea that - we alone are the responsible for the success or failure of the company.

The difficulty level of this step can be diminished by taking an active approach to cultivating, vetting, and then sharing ideas readily and often. It's not so much the shotgun approach where you fire and hope to hit something, but more strategic than that. The approach we are going to take is to be mindful that things can always be improved. As soon as a car manufacturer finishes their current year models, they are already hard at work in designing and conceptualizing what improvements they can make. Companies continue to move forward by becoming better with ideas and execution. Knowing that there is room for improvement in multiple areas gives us an opportunity to find out where we can make the most contribution.

All of this work we are doing is to create something called impact. Impact is where you as person truly feel that you can make a difference. This idea that one individual can impact the fate of 100s of others is where all of this leads to. Believing this truth and letting it become a part of you creates a long-lasting change. The spirit that one person can make a difference allows you to believe more is possible.

Take this outside of work for a moment and think about the change that you can create in the world. If you are able to learn to make a small change where you work, you naturally build the confidence to make bigger impact outside of your job. Confidence comes from successful references. In other words when we achieve the goals you set for yourself, it becomes much easier for you to believe that you are capable of more.

Inside of this chapter we will reflect on three areas. These include accountability, continuous improvement, and impact.
The guiding questions in this chapter are framed to put you into a place of real authority and power. You may not be the CEO or the creator of the company you are in, but with these questions you can develop your own meaningful influence. While answering the questions you need to know your gifts and who would benefit most from them. Most importantly you need to know how to connect.

Guiding Questions on Impact

What individuals suffer the most if I fail?

The question has to be asked. What happens if you fail? With any type of larger than normal effort there is a chance that you won't hit the objectives you set out for yourself. Maybe, the goal you set is too big. Or maybe you haven't yet become the type of person you need to be to complete the mission you created. Even if we give it our very best effort, show up every fucking day, and still don't finish what we set out to do it's not over.

Let's say over the past couple of months you got motivated to exceed the norms. You have been creating a project that you believe will bring in more business for yourself and the rest of the company. Every week you set aside extra time to really dive in to this new goal. The best part about the new goal you set for yourself is how much more motivated you feel. Instead of dragging through your workdays you feel a surge of creativity. You have a strong end goal in mind and have even pitched the early idea to your teams, manager, and an executive that has buy in. This is something that you are going to be presenting at a business unit meeting to about 30-40 people. The project you are working on is a scalable presentation that with the help of others can be used as webinar that generates inbound leads.

The day before the presentation, you prep relentlessly. And everything goes well, you are confident that things are going to move forward. A day later you get called into your managers office, she congratulates you a well-executed presentation but has some bad news. Unfortunately, the other team's leader doesn't want to use your presentation as an inbound strategy. All of the hard work ends up being for not.

The question is: did you fail?

No- absolutely not. In fact, this isn't a failure in any way as everything done in the scenario above are direct steps to making progress. You can't fail if you show up with intention to do your best as often as you possibly can.

The way we are defining failure for this question is the failure to show up. Failing can only happen when you give up yourself. When you stop believing what you are capable of and let others decide what your fate is. There are lots of people who have resigned themselves to this life, wishing and hoping that something changes. This is what true failure is—not trying to live up to your potential. However, trying something new but not hitting the goal isn't failing, its learning. It's progress.

Going back to the question, who would suffer most if you decided that you weren't going to try anymore? Think about the people in your life who know you are capable of great things. How would it affect them if they knew that you were throwing the towel in on yourself?

The heart of this question is really to get you to think about why it's important that you show up as best as you can as often you can.

It's inevitable to have bad days, weeks, or even months. Life can be fickle like that sometimes. Even when circumstances aren't ideal, knowing that you are doing your best is all that matters. Constantly ask this question when you are struggling to get motivation. Recalling on the most important people in your life will help you to find the will power to keep fighting the good fight.

There are people in your life that are counting on you. Maybe, it's your family, your spouse, your kids, or even a friend you are fighting for. Think about the people who might look up to you. Are there individuals in your life that come to you for advice? How would it feel to them knowing you are folding it in.

Now take the time to reflect on the people in your life who matter to you. Get deep on this one and allow yourself to connect emotionally to the possible outcomes, good and bad. The more you can make the goals you set for yourself matter to those that you care about – the more likely you are to not allow yourself to give up.

What are the daily actions I can take to get 1% better?

All of the questions, all of the insights you may have gained throughout this book won't mean anything if action isn't taken. Sometimes the hardest part of making any progress is knowing what to do next. The context of this section is to help you come up with habits and routines to keep progress from getting stale. It's easy to get quick boats of motivation from outside sources such as videos, podcasts, and even books but to sustain that energy you need to create routines and habits that serve you.

The best part about goal setting is the energy and excitement comes from the goal setting itself. Think about it, when you set a goal or have a mindset shift about what's possible the motivation levels are at an all-time high. In fact, the day after you come up with a meaningful goal, you'll probably have a bit more pep in your step. There seems to be an immediate boost the minute you get clear on what is you want. You find yourself working with a new vigor toward the target(s) you set for yourself.

What happens after months of spirit is the boost of extraordinary energy wares off. The nature of humans is to get excited about novelty while adapting to routine. Which is why it's so smart to create a routine that helps you progress in a powerful way. Ideally, the best routines become an automatic set of habits that help you to get in the same energetic, confident, and ambitious state where you can think at your best.

The point of asking this question is for you think about what you want to become and the tiny steps you need to take to get there. With an end goal in mind you can easily determine what habits you need to incorporate into your life to become great. If we ask this question in the right way, we can also create better daily mental states.

While the question we are asking here is **"What are the daily actions I can take to get 1% better".** You can consider rephrasing it in a way that will help you come with the insights you desire most. Such as:

What are the daily actions I can take to have 1% more meaning in my life?

What are the daily actions I can take to be 1% more confident?

What are the daily actions I can take to be 1% more powerful?

First comes the intention then comes the action. Once you really hone in on what it is that you want to be, become, or improve at you can come up with actions that would get you there. You can think about what people who have what you want are doing and how you can incorporate some of their actions into your own life. For example, let's say that the question I ask myself is "What are the daily actions I can take to be 1% more confident" ...here are some of the first action steps that come to mind. The more you time you allow to brainstorm 'what could give me more confidence' the more creative your answers might be.

To be 1% more confident every day, here are some habits that I might be able to implement:
Strong Affirmations about how I want to feel
Writing about feeling confident
Daily Visualization habit
Small challenges outside of normal comfort zone – Chat with a stranger
Sing with my window down
Incorporate the mantra 'Act as If'

Throughout this book we've talked about constantly improving by asking ourselves questions that cause us to think in a new way. When we ask the questions, we can come up with the insights to move us in the desired direction.

When I leave what is the "mark" I want to leave on this place?

Leave a mark with long lasting impact. A mark is something that you become known for, while an impact is defined as "having a strong effect on something". The mark you make is going to be unique to you. To really make it stick it has to be something that benefits people in some way long after you are gone.

How do you make impact that is long lasting beyond your time? It's another one of those tough questions that is not exactly easy to answer. It can be scary to think about depending on where you are in your own journey. Keep this in mind "if it were easy, everyone would be doing it". All of the powerful reflection we've done in this text is here to help us push ourselves to the highest potential.

For this question we want to start thinking about what we can strongly impact in our environment. The most important part of asking these types of questions is aligning them as authentically as we can with what is true to our core values, strengths, and passions.

Values are what we believe as truth with an unwavering, unflinching, and self-assured conviction. A core value for you could be something like I believe every person deserves an equal opportunity to be heard. While another person could have a totally different core value that says I believe that strongest voices know how to make themselves heard. The beautiful thing about a core values is that they sit deep inside us and are our truths. Often, we connect most deeply with people who share similar core values.

Strengths are the areas of ourselves that are naturally or intentionally strong. We've talked about these in Step 2: Find your own enjoyment, but it will be good to resurface these to help create an identifying mark. Strengths could be skills or characteristics that just seem to come easier to us. Some individuals are really strong communicators and seem to connect with people quite easily. Other are strongly analytical. They can take even those most conceptual theories and are able to deeply dissect them in a useful way. Strengths of course can vary, but those who are able to most strongly identify theirs can make the most of them.

Passions get us back to excitement, energy and enthusiasm. These are things we like to do and seem to resonate most strongly with our being. A passion is anything that lights you up inside. These could be particular tasks that you enjoy working on or love to learn about. Passion is where the heart lies, it's a true expression of what you love. A lot of people seem to get stuck on "finding a passion" because they believe that a passion has to radiate so strongly within you that there is no question about what is. That type of thinking can leave many feeling disappointed that they haven't found that "thing". A better way to think about passion is to go back to Step 2: Find your own enjoyment, and ask what energizes me? That's it. If you feel even a mild buzz of additional excitement from a certain activity or task you can start putting that in the passion bucket. Passion is something that can be cultivated and grown over time.

Putting it all together. We want to know how can we take our values, strengths and passions to make impact? To do that we simply ask ourselves how can I combine: what I care about with what I'm good at with what I like doing. That's it, that is the frame work for making impact to others around you.

Answering this question takes serious self-awareness (which is the point of answering these questions). As you continue to use this framework to ask yourself good questions, you will uncover and learn more about yourself. Soon you will be able to combine all that you've uncovered about yourself into a real personal power. Ideally, you can take what you know about yourself and use it to significantly impact those around you.

The reason it's so important to align our ambitions with our authentic selves is because our legacy won't last unless we do. A shallow pursuit of some kind of pseudo fame via being 'known' for something doesn't create a lasting legacy. What we are after with this frame work is to bring to life the greatness inside of us. With the right awareness of who we are, what we are good at, and what we like; We will be able to create a long lasting and significant impact on the world.

Actions and Habits: Impact

The Habits and Actions section is to help you take actionable steps based on the reflections you've done in the previous sections. The "Impact" actions and habits are designed to promote the highest level of contribution. The activities here will help you creating something that is long lasting. Increase your value in an authentic way by committing to these challenges.

These steps along with a PDF with all of the chapter's questions can be downloaded at PinegroveZen.com/tools

Creating Impact Habit #1: Courageous Idea Sharing

Have you ever had a good idea pop into your head, but you don't do anything about it? This habit if implemented successfully will turn you into somebody who confidently, and readily shares your ideas with others. By doing this again and again, as a habit, you will not only be more creative but be seen as someone that has good ideas. The practice of creating new ways of looking at things then sharing them with courage gives you a feedback point that can be used to make the necessary adjustments for the next idea.

The habit we are going to create is the habit of courageous idea sharing, which means you are going to build repetition around creating ideas and then sharing them with others so they can be vetted. It's simple enough in theory but incorporates a couple of skills that add value to your character.

When you create a habit around creating ideas, sharing them, and then taking them on to next level to be vetted a couple of great things are happening.

First, the intention to create an idea that is sharable puts more originality into your system. It allows you to ask questions such "What if we did it like this..." or "What would happen if we framed it like this..." and ... "How could we connect more with ...". Simple questions and what if scenarios leave answers open to a wide range of ideas.

Next, in order to share an idea, you have to be courageous and a bit bold. Especially if you have an idea that you think might directly help somebody else. A great way to approach someone about an idea you have about something they spend all of their time with is... tactfully. In other words, you must learn how to be sensitive to how others may feel about what can be perceived as a critique. This is such an important skill set to learn if you want to lead. Its empathy, sensitivity, and tact all in one. To summarize the act of sharing builds the skill set of tact as well as courage.

Then you get feedback, we could call this the vetting stage. Sharing your ideas with people is one of the most important stages because of the feedback you get from it. When you put your concept out there its pure, untouched, and untested. The person you share this new idea with gets to give you honest and real feedback. This can be painful because of how close you are to your own ideas, but it's a vital step. You also are going to learn how strongly your idea resonates with other people. You may find that no one has buy in to what you are doing. That's ok, take the critiques and modify or move on if you don't feel overly connected to the vision.

The powerful skill learned from this stage of idea sharing is how to take and implement feedback. Each time you share your vision with others and get feedback you learn more and more what resonates and what doesn't. Each idea from that point forward will be even more powerful.

Finally, when you feel you have the right idea and have talked to enough people. It's time to put things in motion. You may be at the execution stage, which is a whole other skill set to learn. Executing is the hardest part of the idea generation stage because it requires work. To work on an idea, you came up with can be extra challenging because now you have to fit this project in with your already busy schedule. Time management is another skill that you will have to master.

Alternatively, you may not be at the execution step and have one more hurdle to cross. This stage usually comes when the feasibility of your idea has been vetted and approved by your peers, but execution requires sign off from someone higher up.

How do you get buy in at the next level? You need to be able to 'sell' the idea. To do this you have to think a couple of positions above. This really forces you to contemplate what it would take to get sign off from someone who is thinking bigger picture. Not only does this help you cultivate strategic, high level thinking, but it also builds your essential sale skills. Ultimately, your ability to execute does come down to your ability to sell your idea. The more authentically passionate you are about the project you are working on, the easier that it will be to sell.

This entire habit of sharing your ideas courageously will help you to grow the following skills:
Creativity
Courage
Handling and Implementing Feedback
Tactful Conversations
Time Management
Selling/Pitching

The beautiful thing about all of this is no matter where your ideas end up, each skill listed above improves with every repetition. So, go out, create and share ideas often. Even if you can't get your ideas off the ground the practice itself is helping you to reach a more well-rounded version of yourself.

Creating Impact Practice: Create your personal powers sheet (Values, Strengths, Passions)

The final practice that we are going to put forth is a practice in pure self-awareness. The goal of this exercise is to create a personal guide that clearly summarizes your unique values, strengths, and passions. After completing this sheet, you will have a short summary of exactly what it is you care most about, what you are naturally strong at, and what truly excites you.

To do this make an appointment on your calendar to set aside an hour of your time. You really want to be able to think through each of these areas to pull up the strongest answers that you can. Ideally, you identify a time of day where you feel the most at peace. This is not something that you necessarily want to do in a rushed or frantic state. The better your state at the time of completing this, the easier it will be. Doing this will create more joy, excitement, and purpose in your life.

Values – Contemplate and answer the questions below to better understand what it is you value.

If I had unlimited money to fix a 'problem' in the world, what would it be?

If I were in charge of my hometown, city, state, or country what are the issues that I would want to fix first?

What are the traits that I most value in others?

Write a Summary about what is that you value. After answering these questions take some time to write a full summary about what you've identified as core values. These are the parts of your being where you feel a deep conviction. Identify what you value by diving into what is you care about, what causes are important, and what it is you value in others.

☐

Strengths – Contemplate and answer the questions below to better understand what is your strengths are

If I were paid for teaching a particular skill what would that skill most likely be?

What are my three strongest attributes?

What types of tasks, assignments, or projects that always seem the easiest for me to complete?

Write a Summary. After answering these questions take some time to write a full summary about what you've identified as your strengths. These include your natural skills, and areas where its easiest for you to learn. Identify what your strengths are by reflecting on past successes or areas of your life where you have been consistently complimented on.

Passions – Contemplate and answer the questions below to better understand what it is your passions are

If I were given an hour every day to learn what every I wanted what would it be?

What subjects have I learned the most about in the past year?

I find myself enjoying these types of activities more than others...

Write a Summary. After answering these questions take some time to write a full summary about what you've identified as your passions. These include the subjects you gravitate towards, and areas that you enjoy learning more about. Identify your passions by thinking about what it is you enjoy doing most without worrying about financial gain.

Final Thoughts

Life can be such a journey and one that you can control with just a bit of intention. Regardless of how closely you follow all of the topics or questions presented in this book, the most important thing to remember is that you have a choice on the path you take.

Advancing in a career path may not be your thing. Not everybody finds fulfillment from working at a high level while gaining increasing levels responsibility. That's ok. Part of the journey here is to figure out what it is that makes you happy. One the best lessons you can take away is how important it is to ask yourself questions that can help you find clarity in your own life.

Most people of us who pick up self-help books are the ones looking for ways to improve. In many cases, we are trying to find answers to questions we have in our own life. The books we read, the videos we watch, and the podcasts we listen to are all attempts to help us resolve areas that we feel some sort of lack from. This lack really comes from comparisons with what we are not. However, one thing to keep in mind is that these gaps come from a perception that we are not where we are.

If we can learn how to redefine our success in a way that takes comparisons away, we will find our self-improvement journey that much more fulfilling. As you continue you to reflect on where you are and where you are going, consider a new metric of success. Instead of making the goal to be something that you are not yet, re-frame the goal as making progress every day toward things that you are authentically excited about. Concentrate your efforts on happily progressing, bit by bit each day. Find the fulfillment in the journey and set your goals based on what's meaningful to you. Don't get caught in the trap of letting others define success for you.

You may not be motivated by becoming financially wealthy, and that is ok. The reason why so many people strive to become millionaires is because of society's perception of success. Remember that when you are setting goals in your own life. Try to pull what's important to you to the surface. Throughout your journey learn to create your own success metrics. Shifting your thoughts of success to what makes you happy allows the challenges you face to really feel like 'opportunities for growth'.

I hope that you will take the time to reflect on what it is you want and answer the questions provided. I really do appreciate you taking the time to read this book. If you enjoyed thinking about the long term in Title Name, you may find a lot of value from my first book called The Happy Cog which focuses on how to create a better day to day approach to your work.

I'd love to connect with you. You can find my other works, blog, and supplemental resources at my website, PinegroveZen.com.

Thank you,
Rob Leo Rando

Made in the USA
Lexington, KY
11 November 2019